PhilanthropyRoundtable

Protecting Your Legacy

A Wise Giver's Guide to Honoring and Preserving Donor Intent

By Joanne Florino with David Bass

Published by The Philanthropy Roundtable, 1120 20th Street NW, Suite 550 South, Washington, D.C. 20036

Free copies of this book are available to qualified donors. To learn more, or to order copies, visit PhilanthropyRoundtable.org, e-mail main@PhilanthropyRoundtable.org, or call (202) 822-8333. Printed versions are available from Amazon. A PDF may be downloaded at no charge at PhilanthropyRoundtable.org.

Cover: Ocskay Bence / Adobe Stock

ISBN 978-0-9978526-3-9
LCCN 2020936365

First printing, May 2020

Current Wise Giver's Guides from The Philanthropy Roundtable

Protecting Your Legacy:
A Wise Giver's Guide to Honoring and Preserving Donor Intent
By Joanne Florino with David Bass

The Fabric of Character:
A Wise Giver's Guide to Supporting Social and Moral Renewal
By Anne Snyder

Uniform Champions:
A Wise Giver's Guide to Excellent Assistance for Veterans
By Thomas Meyer

Learning to Be Useful:
A Wise Giver's Guide to Supporting Career and Technical Education
By David Bass

Catholic School Renaissance:
A Wise Giver's Guide to Strengthening a National Asset
By Andy Smarick and Kelly Robson

Clearing Obstacles to Work:
A Wise Giver's Guide to Fostering Self-Reliance
By David Bass

Agenda Setting: A Wise Giver's Guide to Influencing Public Policy
By John J. Miller and Karl Zinsmeister with Ashley May

Excellent Educators:
A Wise Giver's Guide to Cultivating Great Teachers and Principals
By Laura Vanderkam

From Promising to Proven:
A Wise Giver's Guide to Expanding on the Success of Charter Schools
By Karl Zinsmeister

Closing America's High-achievement Gap: A Wise Giver's Guide to Helping Our Most Talented Students Reach Their Full Potential
By Andy Smarick

Blended Learning: A Wise Giver's Guide to Supporting Tech-assisted Teaching
By Laura Vanderkam

Serving Those Who Served:
A Wise Giver's Guide to Assisting Veterans and Military Families
By Thomas Meyer

Karl Zinsmeister, series editor
For all current titles, visit PhilanthropyRoundtable.org/guidebook

TABLE OF CONTENTS

PREFACE

This new guidebook on protecting donor intent comes at a time when philanthropists are under attack. Some critics declare that philanthropy is, by nature, anti-democratic. Others propose checks on the ability of philanthropists to choose how their gifts will be deployed. Still others attack the concept of donor intent itself, arguing that it is a "dead hand" exerting control from the grave to enforce the original donor's self-serving or outdated wishes, preventing philanthropists from being "held to account."

These critiques have sometimes migrated from blogs and editorials into proposed legislation and regulations that would sharply curb the rights and freedoms of donors. In the mid-2000s, the Senate Finance Committee considered requiring "independent directors" on all private foundation boards, which would have interfered with foundations steered by family members or trusted associates. In 2008, the California Assembly passed legislation imposing demographic disclosure requirements on foundations, with the goal of redirecting gifts to politically favored causes. Similar legislation has been put on the table in other states. Calls to limit the charitable deduction to gifts that provide direct assistance to poor people, or follow other prescribed criteria, have introduced notions of "charitable hierarchy"—arbitrarily asserting that some causes are more worthy than others. Legislators and attorneys general in states across the country are advancing donor disclosure requirements that violate the First Amendment right to privacy in giving. The September 2019 wealth tax proposal of Emmanuel Saez and Gabriel Zucman—both of whom advised several 2020 Presidential candidates—urged that private foundations should be taxed "until the time such funds have been spent or moved fully out of the control of the donor."

At The Philanthropy Roundtable, we believe that private philanthropy is an essential element of American freedom, and central to our greatness as a nation. The voluntary nature of charitable giving, and the sprawling diversity of individual interests it reflects, lie at the heart of cultural innovation in America. Respecting donors' intentions for their gifts is an essential prerequisite for continued charitable giving, and for preventing giving from becoming homogenized and manipulated. Our flourishing, community-building philanthropy is utterly dependent on keeping the trust of voluntary donors, during and after their lifetimes. Our charitable laws, regulations, and practices should support donor intent. Those charged with carrying out donors' wishes bear an ethical obligation to do so to the best of their ability. And in a pluralistic democracy, where citizens are free to make their own decisions about the best ways to improve the well-being of society, the voluntary actions taken within civil society must be protected.

Donor intent is a moral issue, demonstrating respect for individual differences and choices. When we speak of protecting donor intent, we are not referring to a slavish adherence to minute details, but rather to a commitment to honor a donor's principles, to maintain the integrity of his or her philanthropy over time. Donors must make their values and intentions very clear in their mission statements and in their interactions with governing boards and grantees. And those entrusted to carry out the details should be faithful to that trust.

To people suggesting that philanthropic gifts are "public money" because they receive government "subsidies" in the form of tax deductions and exemptions, we respond that those tax provisions are, in fact, not subsidies, but rather vital civil-liberty protections that insulate private giving from government control (though not from reasonable regulation). Evelyn Brody and John Tyler recognized this in our 2012 publication *How Public is Private Philanthropy?*, noting that "with the charitable deduction, the donor, not the government, decides whether to give at all, in what amounts and forms, to which qualified charities, and whether any designations or restrictions accompany the contributions." There are also vital Constitutional reasons to resist the nostrum that charitable gifts should be governmentally controlled—see "Why is Charitable Activity Tax-Protected? (Think Freedom, Not Finances)" in *The Almanac of American Philanthropy.*

We hope that this guidebook encourages donors to think carefully about how they deploy their gifts, and provides them with useful guidelines for making sure their philanthropy accomplishes the good they intend.

Adam Meyerson
President, The Philanthropy Roundtable

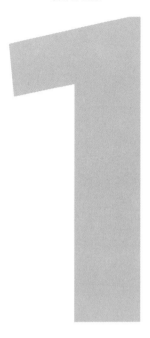

An Introduction to Donor Intent

Born in the second year of the Civil War, Julius Rosenwald played an outsized role in elevating the education available to African-American children in the South during the Jim Crow era. An unlikely philanthropist, Rosenwald spent his early career working in New York City's garment industry making ready-to-wear men's suits. He eventually opened his own clothing store in Chicago and by age 30 had acquired sufficient capital to invest in Sears, Roebuck. His involvement with Sears increased and the store's successful stock offering in 1906 made him a very wealthy man. From 1908 until 1924 Rosenwald served as the company's president and remained its chairman until his death in 1932.

Rosenwald's philanthropic interests were wide-ranging and included Jewish cultural and theological institutions, social-service charities, and affordable housing in Chicago. He was the founding donor of the city's Museum of Science and Industry, and a patron of the University of Chicago. He is most remembered, however, for his work with Booker T. Washington to build—over a 20-year period—nearly 5,000 elementary and secondary schools for black children.

Rosenwald's monetary gifts were themselves extraordinary, but his continued influence among donors derives from the way he practiced his philanthropy. Encouraging "a personal interest by the donor in all activities to which he contributes," he gave his time and talent, as well as his treasure, to the causes he favored. Opposed to handouts, he believed that beneficiaries should be encouraged to help themselves. In his school-building program he required that his donations be matched by local residents (most of whom were poor black families) and by state and county education authorities. He embraced a "give while you live" ethic, stipulating that his own foundation close within 25 years after his death. He opposed perpetual endowments that distributed only a small percentage of their corpus each year and gave so aggressively to his "Rosenwald Schools" that he made both an immediate and enduring impact. By the time of his death, 36 percent of all black children in the still-segregated South were educated in one of the schools he built.

While other donors of his era may have agreed with his principles— Andrew Carnegie, for example, famously wrote, "The man who dies rich, dies disgraced"—they didn't take as many concrete steps to abide by them. Rosenwald believed that a wise donor should focus on his generation's pressing problems, leaving future philanthropic decisions to the judgment of those who would follow. He passed away in 1932 and the Rosenwald Fund closed its doors in 1948, nine years ahead of the schedule he designed. Rosenwald left behind many blueprints for other wise donors to follow.

John Olin was one such donor. Increasingly troubled by a growing anti-business atmosphere among college students and their professors on many campuses in the late 1960s, Olin was determined to counteract that trend. In his 2002 article, "Switching Off the Lights at the Olin Foundation," former Olin Foundation president Jim Piereson noted that John Olin "was greatly influenced by Julius Rosenwald, an early advocate of the idea that foundations should spend their assets within a generation of their donor's demise." Olin understood that by sunsetting his foundation in that timeframe, he would accomplish two goals: ensure that his intent would be fulfilled by trustees who knew him personally and understood and respected his values, and concentrate his charitable gifts over a relatively short period of time to maximize his impact on the conservative and libertarian causes he cherished.

Both Rosenwald and Olin worried about how their charitable dollars might be used after they were gone. Both gave careful consideration to those who would serve on their foundation boards, and both understood that over the long term, successor trustees might not carry out their wishes. Both tackled big and complex issues, and both strategized about maximum effectiveness and early impact. These priorities ultimately led each to limit the life of his foundation.

Perpetuity and donor intent at the Duke Endowment

Sunsetting may be the single best way to prevent a charitable endowment from drifting away from the donor's intent, but it is not the only option. There are foundations set up to exist in perpetuity whose founders took precautions to protect donor intent. The Duke Endowment is a useful example. James Buchanan Duke made his fortune in tobacco and hydroelectric generation in the late nineteenth and early twentieth centuries. When he established a foundation in 1924 with $40 million, his trust limited his philanthropy to North and South Carolina, and directed that grantmaking focus on hospitals, orphan care, rural Methodist churches, and four colleges (Duke University, most notably)—all areas that carried deep personal meaning for him. He even delineated the percentages of annual giving for each area. He entrusted the governance of his philanthropy to his closest personal and business associates, left clear guidelines for the selection of future trustees, and provided for their compensation as a way to bind them—both morally and financially—to the performance of their duties as defined in the indenture.

Since J. B. Duke's death in 1925, the Duke Endowment has distributed more than $1.4 billion. All of its grants fall into the same categories—and largely abide by the same percentages—established by the creator nearly 100 years ago. A century of economic and social change, however, has challenged the trustees and staff to make new meaning of some of their founder's specific instructions. Early grantmaking to orphanages, for example, has evolved into support for foster care, adoption, and programs for children at risk of abuse and neglect. The donor's concern for the health of Carolinians, which once meant only capital grants for hospitals, is today manifested in funding to bring health care to the underserved through home visits and rural clinics. Yet it is still J. B. Duke's original intent that guides the endowment in making these adaptations.

Anticipating his trustees' possible need for some flexibility, Duke included in his indenture of trust a provision allowing them to redirect funds "for the benefit of any such like charitable, religious or educational purpose within the State of North Carolina and/or the State of South Carolina." Far more important, he included an explanation of his reasons for choosing the endowment's specific beneficiaries. "I have included orphans in an effort to help those who are most unable to help themselves," he wrote in one instance. In another he expressed his hope that

> Examples abound of philanthropists
> whose charitable intentions
> were disregarded over time.

"adequate and convenient hospitals are assured…with especial reference to those who are unable to defray such expenses of their own." The Duke Endowment trustees continue to meet ten times annually, as J. B. Duke stipulated. And at one meeting each year, they read the full text of the indenture aloud. The donor's voice and values remain a constant guide in their decisions.

When donor intent is lost
Stories abound of philanthropists whose charitable intentions were disregarded over time—in some instances while they were still living. The names are familiar: Carnegie, Ford, MacArthur, Pew, Rockefeller. And each tale is largely the same. Great tycoons earn wealth through entrepreneurial endeavor before turning their skills and knowledge to the world of philanthropy. Most give to religious and cultural institutions that emphasize right-of-center ideals: faith, patriotism, free enterprise, charity grounded in the hand-up (not handout) ethic, liberty, and personal responsibility. Yet within a generation or two, these donors' philanthropic dollars are diverted to causes alien to their own values.

In some cases, the donors themselves made crucial missteps. Often cited as one of the most egregious violations of donor intent, the Ford Foundation's swing to left-wing grantmaking led to Henry Ford II's resignation from the board of trustees in 1976. Hardly a conservative himself, Ford nonetheless felt compelled to pen a powerful resignation letter that charged the liberal foundation staff with having no understanding of capitalism, the very system that produced the foundation's considerable resources. But at the core of the dispute was a common example of donor neglect. Neither Henry Ford nor his son Edsel, who established the foundation, left clear directives on how its vast wealth should be used. The language in the charter included only the broad, non-specific directive "to administer funds for scientific, educational and charitable purposes, all for the public welfare." The problem was compounded after the deaths of both Edsel and Henry Ford when Henry Ford II relinquished family control of the foundation, making his vote equal to that of any other trustee.

> A shift away from honoring donor intent
> is the natural drift if left unchecked.

John MacArthur left no instructions at all, vague or otherwise, for his foundation's trustees. And Carnegie, who had so clearly expressed in his 1889 *The Gospel of Wealth* a faith in free enterprise, limited government, and self-reliance, failed to embed these values in the Carnegie Corporation. Instead he wrote, "no wise man will bind Trustees forever to certain paths, causes or institutions. I disclaim any intention of doing so. On the contrary, I give my Trustees full authority to change policy or causes hitherto aided, from time to time, when this, in their opinion, has become necessary or desirable. They shall best conform to my wishes by using their own judgment." John D. Rockefeller defined his mission so broadly—"to improve the well-being of mankind throughout the world"—that almost any philanthropic decision would suffice.

J. Howard Pew did spell out his charitable intentions. A religious and political conservative, he ensured that the charter of his philanthropy—the J. Howard Pew Freedom Trust, one of seven family trusts that collectively formed the Pew Charitable Trusts—included a mission statement that clearly delineated his core principles and objectives. Founded in 1957, that trust was intended "to acquaint the American people with the evils of bureaucracy and the vital need to preserve a limited form of government in the United States... the values of a free market...the paralyzing effects of government controls on the lives and activities of people...and...the struggle, persecution, hardship, sacrifice, and death by which freedom of the individual was won." For a period of time, the Pew Charitable Trusts funded conservative and libertarian organizations including Grove City College, the Christian Freedom Foundation, and the American Enterprise Institute. But as the original founders of the Trusts died and professional staff played a larger role in grant decisions, support for the causes dear to J. Howard Pew disappeared. By 1991, the trusts had "eliminated almost all of their right-wing grantmaking and embraced a broad range of projects, including some that manifestly oppose the business interests the old Pews held inviolable," wrote Roger Williams in *Foundation News*. When Pew transitioned in 2003 from a grantmaking foundation to a public charity, all the constituent trusts—including the J. Howard Pew Freedom Trust—were abolished.

Advice on donor intent from philanthropists and experts

As Thomas Tierney and Joel Fleishman write in *Give Smart: Philanthropy That Gets Results*, "Clarifying your values is...the best way we know to ensure that your philanthropy will continue to express what matters most to you. The specific priorities you establish today may evolve and change over the course of time. But deep personal values tend to persist and, as a result, they can provide a continuing touchstone throughout a lifetime of philanthropy. If you establish a foundation intended to last in perpetuity, explicitly clarifying your values will make it far more likely that your foundation will continue to embody and act on them long after you've left the stage."

A shift away from honoring donor intent is often the natural drift, if left unchecked. Heather Templeton Dill, president of the John Templeton Foundation and granddaughter of the original wealth creator (Sir John Templeton), says that the foundation experienced some pressure to reconsider aspects of donor intent when her grandfather passed away in 2008. Linda Childears, former president of the Denver-based Daniels Fund, agrees that efforts to derail donor intent are often sudden and aggressive. "Once the person who earned the original wealth is gone,"

Separating donor intent and grant compliance

Donor intent, properly understood, is distinct from grant compliance. Donor intent is concerned with ensuring that the wealth of a philanthropy's founding benefactor is distributed in a manner consistent with his or her wishes. It operates on a macro-level, concerned with overall fidelity to a wealth-creator's vision. Grant compliance, in contrast, is focused on the micro-details of individual grants and whether a grantee is following the specific terms of a grant agreement.

The distinction between these two concepts is not always obvious, and sometimes the terms are used interchangeably. Both donor intent and grant compliance involve a relationship of trust—the former between an original donor and his heirs and succeeding trustees, and the latter between a donor and her grantees.

she observes, "the people in power—whether that be family or future boards—tend to forget where the wealth came from."

Deviations from donor intent can be less dramatic and dangerously subtle. Lack of clarity about how donated assets are to be used is often the primary culprit in donor-intent violations. Most deviations from donor intent are not the result of conspiracy or malice but are the consequence of largely preventable issues like ill-conceived plans for leadership succession, or unclear, inadequate, or contradictory instructions. To keep your resources dedicated to the causes you care about the most, it's essential that you take pains to define your mission and safeguard the means of carrying it out. You may assume that those who follow will be able to discern your wishes, following the observation of the late Judge Robert Bork in *Donor Intent: Interpreting the Founder's Vision*: "Even where a donor has not made his intentions explicit, it will usually be possible, perhaps within a wide range but a range nevertheless with limits, to determine from his life and activities what uses he would not approve." In reality, too few successors make this effort. The trail of breadcrumbs you leave will often be obscured by the winds of change.

Why donor intent matters

The roots of private giving in the United States go deep and have been continuously nourished by the generosity of individuals who voluntarily utilize their knowledge, creativity, and financial resources for the benefit of others. Philanthropy—large and small—has been a vital force throughout the American experience and reflects the nimble responsiveness of civil society to problems and needs in our smallest towns and around the world. It should be no surprise that a nation founded on individual rights and responsibilities should experience a growth of wondrously diverse independent institutions, important cultural entities that touch our lives every day.

In this context, fidelity to a donor's intent reflects both our respect for individual choice and our gratitude that personal wealth has been set aside to serve the public good. On the flip side, deviations from and deliberate violations of donor intent will inevitably dampen the generosity of donors, who become reluctant to give out of fear that their wealth will be used for causes not of their choosing. This affects philanthropy broadly, notes Tom Riley, president of the Connelly Foundation in Philadelphia: "Our American system thrives in a way that other systems don't because of charitable giving—these institutions of civil society, this enormous nonprofit sector, that provides so much of what's good and appealing about American life. But when donor intent is undermined, it has a chilling effect on giving. That's not just bad for the person—that's bad for everybody."

Taking steps to protect your donor intent is thus an essential and deeply personal undertaking that will pay dividends now and in the future. "My giving is my creation, really," says donor Frances Sykes of the Pascale Sykes Foundation. "I talk about it the way some people talk about their grandchildren. It's part of me." Donor intent—when well-articulated and faithfully observed—will establish the culture and effectiveness of your foundation. "It is the touchstone for how board and staff members ensure the foundation acts according to the right values," says Cheryl Taylor of the Foellinger Foundation. "It's where we start. It guides everything."

Planning ahead

The goal of this guidebook is to help you, and those you bring along on your philanthropy journey, achieve success in defining and protecting your donor intent. Chapters 2 through 6 and chapters 8-9 focus on donor intent in its broadest terms; chapter 7 discusses the special challenges higher-education donors frequently confront in their grantmaking. We present a range of options and approaches, and suggest ways of defining, securing, and perpetuating your charitable intentions. Your final decisions are, of course, your own, and they should be undertaken with the guidance of expert legal counsel.

Without careful attention, your philanthropy may well deviate from your plans and priorities. It can happen during your lifetime, even while you are personally engaged in your giving, and certainly after you're gone. Staying true to donor intent requires a sort of institutional humility—a set of policies and practices that keep your board and staff grounded in the mission and core guiding principles of your philanthropic endeavor. Protecting donor intent is not about denigrating change, nor does it require rigidity. A philanthropic mission may stay constant while the means to achieve that mission change—continuing to honor donor intent.

> Most deviations from donor intent are not the result of malice, but the consequence of preventable issues.

For too many givers, however, donor intent is an afterthought. Your philanthropy can quite easily slip into a comfortable routine of present-oriented grantmaking, giving minimal thought to legal structure, mission statements, governance, and succession plans. It is understandable that donors are eager to put their money to good work as soon as possible and are consequently reluctant to tackle the more challenging topics: conversations about mortality, core values, and letting go of hard-won assets. This is especially true when those discussions might upset members of extended (or complicated) families. But careful consideration of a range of structures and strategies for securing your philanthropic intentions is a necessary first step for advancing your charitable legacy. In doing that work you are also helping your family, associates, and future directors to understand and carry out the mission you set for them.

For Ingrid Gregg—former president of the Earhart Foundation and currently senior program director at the Lynde and Harry Bradley

Foundation—donor intent is at its core a matter of trust. "There are few things in civil society, or even in organizations, that work well without trust. So the implicit value of all the good that flows in philanthropic giving comes from donors knowing that their wishes, and that the original trust they placed in people, is going to be respected by those who come after them," Gregg remarks. "One of the greatest privileges of working in philanthropy," she adds, "is helping donors achieve their goals when they've worked so incredibly hard to create the resources that they then make available to society."

Defining Your Mission

Whether you intend to spend all funds during your lifetime, sunset your foundation, or establish an entity in perpetuity, a strong, well-crafted mission statement is indispensable. Although the IRS requires only a general statement of charitable intent in a foundation's incorporating documents, donors are wise to include much more. As philanthropic consultant Calvin Edwards notes, "A clear and precise mission statement is the bedrock for protecting donor intent. It all starts there."

A powerful mission statement underpins the crucial decisions you make about the governance and operations of your philanthropy. It leads to greater focus and clarity by helping you discern what is central and what is peripheral to your giving. It enables you to define the geographic boundaries of your generosity, identify board members committed to your objectives, decide whether to involve family members, explain to grantseekers what you will and will not fund, and decline off-mission funding requests. If you intend your philanthropy to last beyond your lifetime, a well-written mission statement helps your future trustees and heirs answer the fundamental question: What would our founder have done in these circumstances?

Crafting your mission statement may take considerable time. Some philanthropists arrive at a mission statement through a trial-and-error approach, learning from past mistakes. Others know exactly what they want to accomplish up front. Regardless, defining a mission is a deliberative process that often requires multiple revisions. Devoting as much attention as necessary to this task is particularly crucial (given the predilections of typical philanthropic staffers) if your philanthropy encompasses conservative or libertarian causes like fostering free markets, individual liberty, and traditional American values. "It's vitally important that such donors specify a mission for their foundations that tells trustees, staff, and successor trustees what they want done with their money. If that's not done, their foundations will become liberal organizations," says Pierson.

Dan Searle understood the value of a mission statement that conveyed not only what he intended his philanthropy to accomplish, but also the values and philosophy behind his actions. Searle's giving initially focused on supporting local Chicago-area institutions—such as the Art Institute, Northwestern University, and the Botanic Garden. Beginning in the mid-1990s, however, Searle decided to reinvent his philanthropy, creating the Searle Freedom Trust to focus exclusively on advancing liberty.

Well aware of the proclivity of philanthropies to veer off course over time, Searle employed Kim Dennis (who served as president of The Philanthropy Roundtable from 1991 to 1996) to help him craft a mission statement defining his donor intent. That inaugurated a six-month-long process of back-and-forth between Searle and Dennis. He asked her to collect mission statements from other foundations that had successfully preserved donor intent, like the Bradley Foundation. To illustrate his philosophy and outlook, he shared books he admired and clippings from the *Wall Street Journal* and other publications that resonated with him.

To hone his new foundation's focus areas, Searle talked extensively with Dennis, and the two of them met with representatives from freedom-advocating think tanks and other institutions to garner their input.

Eventually, Dennis developed a first draft, which Searle then further refined over a process of several months. "By the end of the process," Dennis says, "there wasn't a single word in there that wasn't intentional. It's only a six-page document, but every word was there because Dan wanted it there. We had long discussions over whether we should use the word *freedom* or *liberty*, over whether America is a *democracy* or a *democratic republic*. Once he finished it, he never made a change to it."

Aside from canonizing Searle's donor intent in written form, his mission statement served another crucial function: teaching Dennis a great deal about Searle's thinking process. That was a critical factor in maintaining donor intent after Searle passed away in 2007 and Dennis became president of the trust. When trustees and staff work side-by-side with a donor they develop a much more nuanced understanding of the individual's motivation, core values, and problem-solving strategies. Today, the Searle Freedom Trust has a robust portfolio of grantees that share Dan Searle's goals for his philanthropy: "creating an environment that promotes individual freedom and economic liberty, while encouraging personal responsibility and a respect for traditional American values."

Another example of a mission statement comes from the Lovett and Ruth Peters Foundation based in Cincinnati, Ohio. Lovett Peters made his fortune in the energy industry in the mid-twentieth century. He and his wife Ruth shared the same philanthropic passion. "They believed the best legacy they could leave behind was to try and help all Americans receive a great education, especially those most in need," says Dan Peters, their son who serves as president of the Peters Foundation.

Shortly after establishing the foundation in late 1993, Lovett Peters sat down and produced a concise mission statement barely over a page in length. "A mission statement doesn't have to be that complicated," Dan Peters says. This statement included a provision that the foundation sunset no more than 30 years after the death of the donors, stated a clear preference for "high-risk" philanthropic gifts with the potential for strong results, and favored supporting new up-and-coming opportunities over well-established programs. In 2000, Ruth and Lovett amended the statement to make clear that the education of children was their first priority.

Dan Peters had the opportunity to work directly with his mother and father on their philanthropic priorities for over a decade before their deaths in 2009 and 2010. He emphasizes the importance of the mission statement—but also the fact that his parents gave during their lifetimes so he could see firsthand how they prioritized their philanthropy. "Giving while living helps you see the roadmap and understand the texture and intent," he says. It is no surprise, then, that the foundation continues to focus on high-leverage investments in K-12 education on a national level.

The Searle and Peters examples demonstrate that developing a mission statement requires repeated refinements, both before grantmaking begins and after a donor gains more experience in foundation operations. Consider Sir John Templeton, who created his foundation in 1987 but updated his charter over a dozen times during the next two decades before stepping down as chairman in 2006. As his granddaughter observes, one of the things Templeton did well was to provide specificity. He called for seven giving areas, established expenditure limits for each, and included guidelines for renewal decisions on grants.

> A well-written mission statement
> will let your successors answer
> the fundamental question:
> What would our founder have done?

Specificity about the "what" of grantmaking, while helpful, is insufficient to guide a foundation in honoring donor intent across generations. Templeton codified what is far more important and instructive—the principles he intended to drive his philanthropy: intellectual humility and open-mindedness, relentless curiosity, and individual and economic freedom. Many of the big questions the Templeton Foundation asks today—Why are we here? How can we flourish? What are the fundamental structures of reality? What can we know about the nature and purposes of the divine?—stem from inquiries the founder made in his own lifetime.

No matter the age of your foundation, it's never too late to create a comprehensive mission statement. Take the example of the Philadelphia-based Connelly Foundation. Prior to 1990—when the foundation's wealth creator, businessman John Connelly, passed away—the foundation had been largely run out of Connelly's checkbook. Connelly never wrote an official mission statement, though he had a strong philanthropic track record reflecting consistent personal views. The foundation was operating, as Riley puts it, on "common law"—unwritten, though widely understood. However, as the foundation's governance began to pass to descendants and trustees who didn't know Connelly personally, the need for a strong, written mission statement became urgent.

"A lot of times, there's an assumption that if your board is comprised of family members or business colleagues or friends who knew the wealth creator well, they'll transmit that knowledge to others through osmosis," says Riley. "That doesn't happen. It only really happens if you make a deliberate effort to codify and distill these principles. If it doesn't get written down in practical terms, it's going to get lost over time."

> There's an assumption that if your board is comprised of family or business colleagues, they'll transmit knowledge of the founder through osmosis. That doesn't happen.

The ingredients of an effective mission statement

Your mission statement should describe—as concisely as possible—the reasons behind your philanthropy. You can then supplement your statement with an addendum that contains more detail: your principles and beliefs, preferred operating principles, grantmaking guidelines, and succession directions. Landing on the best wording for your mission statement can be a long process, but it's well worth the time. Following these steps will help:

Discuss your values and principles

Discussing your values helps future trustees, staff, and family not only know the "what" of your philanthropic giving, but the crucial "why" as well. As she worked to recover and preserve donor intent at the Daniels Fund, Childears regretted that Bill Daniels had not explained his values and beliefs in more detail for future generations to reference. Daniels had clarified his wishes—where he wanted his money to go, down to payout percentages—but he hadn't spent much time on the principles that should govern the foundation's grantmaking.

Although explaining a donor's "what" is crucial, don't stop short there. The "why" is also vital. "When a donor says he wants to work in, say, performing arts, just knowing that is not good enough," Childears warns. "It's why you want us to work in performing arts. What matters to you about it? Is it the audience experience? The cultural value? What specifically about those funding areas matters to you?"

If you're not sure how to talk about your values, here are some questions to get you started:

- What are the ideas, traditions, persons, events, and circumstances that shaped you as a person? How are they reflected in the personal and professional choices you have made in your life?
- What experience have you had with charitable giving and what has given you the most satisfaction? What has disappointed you?
- Why are you establishing a philanthropic entity now? What good are you trying to achieve? What problems do you want to address? Are you working to improve society in general, help a specific segment of the population, benefit a certain geographic area, or support a particular institution?
- Do you want your faith to be reflected in your philanthropy? If so, how?
- Is family involvement in your philanthropy important to you? If so, then carefully spell out who will be involved and what role they will play. (See Chapter 3 for a full discussion of protecting donor intent in family foundations.)
- Are there philanthropists whom you admire? On what grounds?
- Are there nonprofit leaders you admire? Why?
- What are the biggest mistakes you see in philanthropy? How will you avoid repeating them?
- What values do you want to form the basis for your philanthropy? What steps can you take to ensure that others understand and honor those values?
- Are there ideas, institutions, and places that you will not support? "Your mission statement should have negative covenants as well as positive covenants," advises philanthropy consultant Al Mueller.

Use clear language and be specific
Clarity is of utmost importance when you're creating your mission statement. Think about it from the perspective of readers who never knew you

or your philanthropy—would they comprehend your meaning? Would they have an accurate understanding of what motivates you? Would they know not only your grantmaking priorities, but also the outcomes you seek and the strategies you prefer? "Helping the needy" opens the door to any number of grants with which you might disagree. "Enabling the poor to support themselves with dignity through workforce training and character development" identifies both end and means. "This is an outcome at the level of the recipient, not the organization—and that makes all the difference. It focuses on the change you want to see among members of society," says Calvin Edwards, who works with donors to formulate effective giving strategies and assess their impact.

In addition to carefully choosing your language, be specific. Specificity is one of the greatest resources for preserving donor intent through a mission statement. As Riley notes about mission statements, "the most inspiring ones can sound poetic. But they're almost useless." In contrast, useful mission statements are precise. "Say a donor specifies that his foundation's money should support teaching engineering in Kansas, because he was an engineer. Well, that's not a lofty mission statement, but it's going to be hard for future generations to pervert that and spend it on whatever they want."

Make your mission statement readable and memorable. One way to achieve this outcome is to keep it short, and use supporting documentation to elaborate further. "Long mission statements tend to ramble and decrease in clarity with their length," Edwards says. "Pick your verbs carefully and avoid 'weasel' verbs that, it seems, every nonprofit organization in the world uses, such as 'help, equip, empower.' Use more precise verbs than those generic terms."

Identifying operating principles

Now that you've formulated a concise and strong mission statement, the next step is to create supporting documentation surrounding your statement, including the thinking and principles that will guide the operations of your charitable entity. Think through these questions:

- Will you do all your giving in your lifetime? Assign a sunset schedule for your foundation? Plan for perpetuity?
- Will you support direct services to individuals: scholarships, medical care, food banks, and the like? Will you fund cultural institutions like churches, schools, museums, and research

organizations? Or will you effect change through advocacy, public education, policy work, publications? Are you comfortable with some mixture of these? In what ratios?

- Will you support local, regional, or national organizations? Or some combination? Will your strategies and charitable topics differ from one level to another?
- Will you provide start-up support, or do you prefer well-established organizations?
- Will your grantmaking involve fewer large grants, or many smaller grants?
- Will you consider multi-year grants? Matching grants?
- What kind of relationship do you want with grantees? Do you want to give your grantees active guidance and direction? Or do you prefer to let them manage execution themselves?
- Will you support endowments, capital campaigns, or annual galas?
- Will you fund only specific programs or projects? Or will you consider general operating support?
- Will you seek collaborative funding? Public-private partnerships?
- What kind of visibility would you like? Should your entity ever give anonymously? If so, under what circumstances? Should you (or your successors) produce an annual report, maintain a website, or otherwise promote your philanthropy?
- What is your timeframe for achieving desired outcomes? Are you looking for immediate payoffs, or do you prefer to invest for the long term?
- How will you use evaluation and assessment in your grantmaking?
- With your timeframe decision in mind, what sort of spending rate do you prefer—the minimum amount required by law (5% of assets annually for private foundations) or a more aggressive approach?
- How will your assets be invested? Will you consider mission-related investing? Program-related investing?
- Are there types of grants that you absolutely will not make? Funding areas to be avoided? Operating procedures that are unacceptable?

Involving people you trust

Returning to the story of Dan Searle's collaboration with Kim Dennis, some donors will find it most helpful to involve others in formulating a mission statement. These trusted individuals may be family members, professional colleagues, other philanthropists, or nonprofit directors who share your values. You may also decide to bring on a consultant to help. Consider engaging potential trustees or staff members in the conversation.

While the mission statement should reflect your values, talking early on with those who will carry out your intentions will help them better understand you and your donor intent. You may be concerned that conversations with others will only confuse your thoughts, but one anonymous donor found that early discussions reinforced his intentions for his philanthropy. One of his foundation executives explains: "Once we had a document that he was comfortable with, he sent it out to about two dozen people in the foundation world and the policy world. We asked for their reactions to it. People wrote long responses, sometimes several pages long. A lot of people said he should elaborate on some point, but for every person who said to elaborate, we had someone else say the material should be shortened. We incorporated some of the recommendations, but not a lot. He was persuaded by very few of them. But what the process did was give him confidence in the document we had. He found that he liked it the way it was."

> Create materials that convey to others
> your character, passions, goals, and ideas.

Supplementing your mission statement

If you want to add to the documentation of your donor intent, consider creating supplemental materials that convey to others your character, passions, goals, and ideas. You might record a video in which you speak candidly to a sympathetic interviewer about your values, principles, background, and vision. Legacy statements, which are simply more comprehensive mission statements, help transmit donors' sensibilities across time to directors, staff, and family. You may also include notes, letters, and speeches that enable others to capture your personal history as well as the nuance and richness of your intentions. "It's really helpful that my grandfather wrote so much about what he wanted, because we have a lot of text we can refer to," notes Dill.

Donn Weinberg, a former trustee of the Harry and Jeanette Weinberg Foundation, emphasizes the crucial role of the first generation of trustees in preserving the original wealth creator's voice for future generations. "Early generations of trustees have an obligation to create a history, to memorize what the founder not only said, but meant and cared about, liked and didn't like, so that it's a guide for future trustees," he says. "If they don't do that, future trustees really don't have anything solid to guide them, and as a result they fall back on their own discretionary desires."

At the M. J. Murdock Charitable Trust, executive director Steve Moore began shortly after his hiring in 2006 to assemble a wealth of material to understand and document the donor intent of founder Melvin J. "Jack" Murdock. A consummate entrepreneur from his youth, Murdock and a partner eventually launched the electronic instrumentation company Tektronix, Inc., in 1946. Amidst the electronics surge following World War II the company boomed. After Murdock died in a plane crash at the age of 53, his will established a charitable trust "to nurture and enrich the educational, cultural, social and spiritual lives of individuals, families and community."

Although the trust had already been operating for three decades when he was hired, Moore took on the task of assembling a list of people who knew Jack Murdock the best, visiting them, and asking about Murdock's philanthropic wishes. "A whole generation of people who knew Jack firsthand were dying off," Moore recounts. "They were in their 90s, 80s, and some late 70s. And so I hired a videographer to go along with me, and I just interviewed them and asked them to tell me about Jack Murdock—what he valued, what he gave to, what interested him."

Moore and his staff then assembled taped interview clips to provide an audio-visual record of Murdock's donor intent. When Moore sat down with the three sons of Murdock's business partner—who had often gone fishing with Jack—they shared many stories about his passion for the outdoors and conservation (which is a cornerstone funding area of the Murdock Charitable Trust). Videos and oral histories are excellent ways to "embody" donor intent, Moore suggests. "We all learn by stories. A good story illustrates your goals much better than a two-chapter document."

What a great mission statement can—and cannot—do
Violation of donor intent is always a danger—either through an abrupt turning of the ship or through small incremental deviations over an extended period. A well-defined mission statement goes a long way toward preventing that. As Bradley Foundation CEO Richard Graber says, "In many ways, the easy part is putting those words on paper—that's the first part. The second part—the harder part—is executing. But without that first part, I'm not sure you can get to the second part."

The function of a mission statement is assisting those who come after you—whether family members, directors, a court, or beneficiaries—to understand your goals. Yet you still must have successors who desire to carry out your wishes.

By their very nature, the power of mission statements is limited. Even if you supplement your statement with legacy documents, videos, and other supporting materials, these items, while necessary, cannot guarantee that your donor intent will be honored. They put guardrails around donor intent, but the charitable vehicle can still crash. The "people part" of the equation is enormously important.

"I often say our Searle board meetings are more like séances—we're always asking what Dan would have done," Dennis says. "Even though we have this great mission statement, it's less the mission statement that controls us than actually sitting there and remembering Dan, knowing what he would have done. In the end, no document will protect you from people who want to pursue their own ends."

In subsequent chapters this guidebook will discuss other critical elements in protecting donor intent: the timeframe of your philanthropy, the philanthropic vehicle you choose, the governance structure you establish, and—of course—the individuals you bring on board.

Choosing a Timeframe for Donating

In establishing your philanthropy, an immediate priority for preserving your donor intent is considering a timeframe for your giving. There are three potential approaches: disbursing your assets while you live, arranging to "sunset" your giving at a specific time after your death, or creating an entity that will exist in perpetuity. There are advantages and drawbacks to each timeframe. This chapter will help you think through each approach and decide which is best for your circumstances.

Giving it all away while living

The notion of spending much of one's fortune while living is a concept briskly taking hold in philanthropic circles around the globe. Giving away money fast—to do good right now—is an idea championed by some of the most high-impact, high-net-worth donors of the modern era. Philanthropic heavy hitters like Bill and Melinda Gates, Warren Buffett, Mark Zuckerberg and Priscilla Chan, Richard and Joan Branson, Larry Ellison, and Eli and Edythe Broad have all made giving while living a priority. As of early 2020, 207 high-net-worth individuals and couples have signed the Gates and Buffett Giving Pledge, promising to give more than half of their wealth away during their lifetimes—albeit in many cases to foundations that will operate after the donors' deaths.

Many of these philanthropists have drawn inspiration from a donor who has fulfilled his pledge to give everything away in his lifetime. Charles ("Chuck") Feeney, 89 years old when this book comes out, is co-founder of Duty Free Shops. His Atlantic Philanthropies has distributed a total of $8 billion over 35 years. Atlantic Philanthropies concluded nearly all its giving in 2016 and plans to close its doors permanently in 2020, the largest foundation in history to spend itself out of existence.

Feeney's story is highly unusual in the annals of philanthropic giving: With a single stroke in 1982, he divested himself of his fortune and dedicated it to charitable uses, and he did this anonymously. He chose anonymity out of heartfelt modesty, out of concerns about his family's security, out of his entrepreneurial inclination to "kick the tires" of prospective grantees without being recognized, and out of concern that publicity might discourage other donors from giving to the same worthy causes. As Conor O'Clery wrote in *The Billionaire Who Wasn't: How Chuck Feeney Secretly Made and Gave Away a Fortune*, "Feeney's philanthropic model is unique in its combination of size, offshore location, freedom of action, flexibility, anonymity, limited life span, willingness to make big bets, and global impact. It is a philanthropic landmark of the new century."

Feeney's motivation to give in his lifetime was threefold: First, he hoped to dodge the bureaucratic sclerosis that afflicts foundations as they age, seeking instead the nimbleness and "opportunity-driven" engagement he enjoyed in his business. Second, he wanted to maximize the impact of his gifts. "I see little reason to delay giving when so much good can be achieved through supporting worthwhile causes today. If I have $10 in my pocket, and I do something with it today, it's already producing $10 worth of good," says Feeney. Most important of all, he embraced the pure joy of "giving while living," which maximizes both the size of gifts and their pleasures. Indeed, Feeney is perhaps the best spokesperson for the satisfaction derived from generous giving and from seeing with his own eyes the impact made. The man who consistently asked his associates, "What will we have to show for it?" has encouraged other donors to consider giving in their lifetimes, noting that it "has been a rich source of joy and satisfaction for me, and for my family as well." Feeney is also a man who never let himself get attached to money. He is famously known for wearing a $15 watch, insisting on flying coach, and using plastic grocery bags to carry around his belongings. "He has loved making money, but not having it," as O'Clery puts it.

> Giving away money fast—to do good right now—is an idea championed by some of the most high-impact donors of the modern era.

Other donors view the practice of divesting themselves of their wealth during their lifetimes as wise stewardship. "For some reason, God gave me more financial resources than I need or deserve, and therefore I believe I'm supposed to be the one to give them away," says Houston philanthropist David Weekley. "To me, the folks who earn and help create these resources have a responsibility to invest in nonprofit organizations with the same acumen and talents that helped create the resources in the first place." Weekley established a family foundation in 1991 and today works to make grants of nearly $20 million a year. A recent focus for the foundation has been to fund organizations across the globe that encourage human prosperity. For Weekley, this stage in his life demands a new perspective: "It really takes a different mindset that I wasn't prepared to have 10 years ago, or even five years ago. It's time to move to the distribution part of my life cycle. And while I've been distributing in the past, I've still been accruing in terms of my net worth. But now I need and want to start distributing my current net worth, which is different than giving out of income."

One enormous benefit of giving all your wealth away while living is obvious—it effectively eliminates the risk of a violation of your donor intent in the future. When done wisely, it also helps protect donor intent in the present. Even living donors can find themselves frustrated by staff and board members who steer grantmaking in unwelcome directions, and by grantees who ignore the terms of gifts. (For more on this, see chapters 7 and 8.) A diligent and observant living donor focused on effective giving in the here and now is far more likely to ensure that funds are used for appropriate purposes than a donor who bets on a foundation left behind after his or her death.

Most important—as Chuck Feeney and David Weekley understand—giving away your fortune while living enables you to address today's pressing problems, to be directly involved in solutions, and to invest time, wisdom, and business skills in addition to wealth. "Giving while living is the truest form of philanthropy because it's personal," notes Riley. "It's the human-scale connection that's so wonderful and virtuous." Donors who choose the path of giving while living may be choosing the most satisfying path of all.

> He hoped to dodge the bureaucratic sclerosis that afflicts foundations as they age, seeking instead the nimbleness he experienced in business.

Giving while living and time-limiting what remains

Although allocating all your charitable dollars during your lifetime is growing fast in popularity, it doesn't appeal to all donors. Some are focused on problems that will become more acute in the future, or are committed to helping start-up nonprofits that will require decades to reach maturity. Others may simply not have the energy to distribute all their wealth while living. If these factors apply to you, then establishing a grantmaking entity that will survive you for a limited span of time may be the right choice.

Time-limited foundations have grown in appeal in recent decades. Born out of broad concerns over the difficulties of protecting donor intent over a long term, the practice of "sunsetting" is becoming more common. Although the precise number of time-limited foundations is unknown, an analysis by the Bridgespan Group reported that "only 5 percent of the total assets held by America's largest 50 foundations were in spend-down in the early 1960s, compared to 24 percent in 2010." As Riley notes, "25 years ago, sunsetting was a dramatic, unusual thing to do. Today, it's increasingly seen as a best practice. The more sophisticated you become about charitable giving, the more you know the history of charitable giving, the more you experience the many instances of donor intent gone awry, the more sunsetting makes sense."

Sunsetting foundations come in all sizes, and focus on many issues. Bill and Melinda Gates describe themselves as "impatient optimists" when it comes to their philanthropy. There is a sense of urgency in their decision to put their charitable dollars to immediate use on today's needs. They initially planned for the Gates Foundation to close its doors 50 years after both of their deaths, but later shortened the timeframe to 20 years. Giving away their wealth "is the most fulfilling thing we've ever done," said Bill Gates during a 2014 TED talk, and the couple has pledged that 95 percent of their wealth will go to the Gates Foundation.

Bernie Marcus, a co-founder of Home Depot, established his foundation with the stipulation that it sunset 30 years after his death, but has recently reduced that period of time to 20 years. He has purposefully created an age differential on his board so that most members will still be there at the foundation's close. He has also created ironclad parameters around how his money should be allocated. In an interview with the Bridgespan Group he spoke plainly about a time earlier in his life when he asked a member of a foundation board how they made their decisions. The trustee told him the donor had left no instructions, so "we give where we want to give, and even favor organizations the donor would have disliked." For Marcus, the impact was immediate and powerful and led to his determination to avoid the risks of perpetuity in his own foundation. "I don't want people to be here in perpetuity. I think it's a terrible thing to do.... People use that for their own benefit.... You've got to be dumb to let a foundation go on forever."

When Gerry Lenfest made a fortune from the sale of his cable company in 1999, he determined to give away his wealth as quickly and intelligently as possible. The result was more than $1.3 billion in giving during his lifetime (he died in 2018), much of it to the Philadelphia area. "I don't want to die with a lot of wealth," he told *Philanthropy* magazine in 2014. "I don't believe in wealth going on in perpetuity. There are occasions when it's turned out to be well done, but they are few in my opinion." The Lenfest Foundation will sunset in the next decade.

Tom Lewis, a donor from Scottsdale, Arizona, is also following the idea of giving while living. He and his wife Jan are using their "wealth, wisdom, work, and witness to try and make a difference while alive." The T. W. Lewis Foundation focuses on five areas: higher education, helping children and families in need, character education, building community through local organizations, and strengthening America. "A lot of the gifts we've made lead to interesting, meaningful experiences. It's become a kind of new identity for us, a new purpose," says Lewis.

The advantages of time-limiting your philanthropy

For donors committed to protecting their intent, time-limited foundations have a distinct advantage over philanthropic entities that exist in perpetuity. As a living donor, you have already established a pattern of grantmaking, and you have chosen board members who work with you in that process. Although not foolproof, having the bulk of your charitable giving take place in your lifetime gives you direct oversight, and leaves behind an imprint to guide any further disbursements—"a record that puts donor intent on a practical basis and that can be cited in the future when questions arise," as Jim Piereson puts it.

The Searle Freedom Trust in Washington, D.C., is steadily spending down toward closure by the year 2025. "Our sunset makes me confident that we're going to do what Dan Searle wanted to do—we will stick to his mission through the end," says Dennis. "I would not be confident of that if we were going beyond that end date. Right now, everyone involved with the foundation knew Dan, and as that changed, people just wouldn't have the same feeling of responsibility to the donor."

The Detroit-based Ralph C. Wilson Jr. Foundation is also benefitting from a board of trustees who knew the original wealth creator well. Before he passed away in 2014, Ralph Wilson handpicked four trustees (including his wife, Mary Wilson) and charted a 20-year sunset timetable. "Ralph had seen how the Ford Foundation left Detroit [for New York City, in 1953] and that really bothered him," Mary Wilson told *The Chronicle of Philanthropy* in July 2018. "He wanted to make sure that the people who knew him best, and the ones that he had total confidence in, were part of this." Wilson's foundation is now busily spending itself out of existence—a big chore given the over $1 billion infusion of cash it received after the sale of Wilson's Buffalo Bills NFL football team. The foundation is the largest philanthropic engine in western New York and among the largest in southeast Michigan (the foundation's two target areas). Although Wilson left no specific instructions for how to spend his money beyond the general welfare of those communities, he put trusted people in place to carry out his legacy in alignment with his values, within a limited timeframe.

A second advantage of sunsetting is the outsized philanthropic impact you can have through aggressive spending while heading toward a closing date. Dan Peters, who is charged with spending all funds from his parents' Lovett and Ruth Peters Foundation by no later than 10 years after his death, is finding it "liberating." The spend down gives the foundation leeway to extend its giving far behind the 5 percent annual distribution that most permanent foundations follow. "The need is now—why wait?" Peters says.

The Pascale Sykes Foundation in New Jersey plans to spend itself out of existence by 2023 at the latest. Donor Frances Sykes founded the philanthropy in 1992 to help low-income families in some of the poorest New Jersey counties. Initially established in perpetuity, Sykes and her trustees voted just four years later to time-limit, specifically for reasons of donor intent. In 2012, Sykes convened an ad hoc group of New Jersey nonprofits, faith-based organizations, researchers, and government officials to create a 10-year spend-down plan. Sunsetting has added focus and urgency to her grantmaking, Sykes says. "Sunsetting is hard work—it's not for sissies," she admits. "It's much easier to chug along and spend 5 percent each year. But when you're sunsetting, you have to think entrepreneurially. You have to see the need, the demand. You have to see if your giving does the job. You go with what works."

The Roy Lichtenstein Foundation chose the unusual spend-down path of liquidating a significant portion of its art collection by donating it to the Whitney Museum and the Smithsonian. Roy Lichtenstein was one of the twentieth century's most famous pop artists, known for his comic-book-style work. "I like the idea of handing it off," his widow Dorothy Lichtenstein told the *New York Times*. "I don't want to leave things up in the air." The foundation is continuing to allocate its remaining artwork to museums in America and Europe. "We have always intended that the foundation, now almost 20 years old, would not operate in perpetuity, and are delighted we can create a new way forward with our first set of chosen successor institutions, well before we 'sunset,'" Lichtenstein has stated.

The William E. Simon Foundation, a family philanthropy based in New York City, helps inner-city households access education and community services that foster personal success and self-reliance. Its founder, former Treasury Secretary William Simon, also served as president of the John M. Olin Foundation and as a trustee of the John Templeton Foundation. Emulating John Olin, Simon stipulated that his foundation sunset within a few decades of his death. Originally scheduled to close its doors by 2029, the foundation is now likely to sunset in 2023 or 2024 because of its board's decision to spend more aggressively in its final years.

In one of the better-known early examples of spend-down, the Aaron Diamond Foundation spent itself out of existence by 1996. The foundation was funded in 1985 after the death of real-estate developer Aaron Diamond two years prior. Aaron and his wife, Irene, had decided to allocate all their resources over the course of one decade to have the greatest possible impact—in this case, on the AIDS epidemic. Their foundation became the largest private supporter of AIDS research in the U.S., devoting $220 million to the New York City-based Aaron Diamond AIDS Research Center whose pathbreaking scientific work ended up saving millions of lives.

Sunsetting needn't be a rigid process. "When the subject of sunsetting is first broached, it can seem pretty final and dramatic," says Riley. "It doesn't have to be abrupt. You can do it over a period of time, the grantees anticipate it, and can plan accordingly." As sunsetting grows in popularity, more spend-down foundations are publicizing their experiences and leaving behind their "roadmaps" for others to follow.

When boards decide to sunset

The decision to sunset is sometimes made by trustees after the original wealth creator has passed away. For example, the New York City-based Avi Chai Foundation sunsetted in 2019 as a result of a decision made six years after Zalman Bernstein's death. Bernstein founded Avi Chai in 1984 with a two-fold mission: Jewish education and Jewish unity. The foundation has made grants in North America, Israel, and the former Soviet Union to support Jewish day schools, connect secular and religious Jews around a shared heritage, and promote Jewish thinking in the public sphere.

Bernstein never specifically requested a spend-down for the foundation, but he did communicate the desire informally to trustees, expressing concern about the mission drift of the Ford Foundation and his wish that his philanthropy avoid that fate. Bernstein passed away in 1999, but it

Model donor—
Raikes Foundation

Jeff and Tricia Raikes provide another example of giving while living. Jeff Raikes served as CEO of the Gates Foundation between 2008 and 2014, and worked for Microsoft Corporation 27 years as a member of the senior leadership team. Tricia Raikes served as the company's director of creative services and marketing communications.

They created their own foundation in 2002 and have given away over $100 million since then. They focus on youth-serving institutions, including those working in education and homelessness. The couple initially created their foundation without a firm timeframe, but later decided to sunset by 2038. They've identified several reasons for doing so: the sense of urgency that it creates, an increased willingness to take risks, the ripple effect their philanthropy can have to inspire and motivate other donors, a foolproof way for the donors' voices to be heard, and elimination of the risk of mission drift in future generations.

One of their most compelling reasons is the personal satisfaction they derive from giving while living. "We're anxious to see positive social changes that stem from our philanthropic investments during our lifetime," Jeff says. "The more we identify and see the joy in the impact our philanthropy can have, the more we're focused, committed, and dedicated. And the more we're focused, committed, and dedicated, the better our philanthropy can be. That center point—the joy of giving, the joy of philanthropic impact—is central to successful philanthropy."

"We certainly do view this as our life work," Tricia adds, "and it certainly is a reflection of us. We try to bring our whole game to work every day. There's just a tremendous sense of satisfaction when work comes to fruition and you can really see how the results are impacting people."

wasn't until around 2005 that the executive committee and the board of trustees made the decision to sunset. Initially, the date was set for January 2027 to honor what would have been Bernstein's 100th birthday. Trustees later moved the date earlier.

Avi Chai's sunset strategy had one distinctive characteristic: Because the foundation decided to retain sufficient funds to make annual grants in perpetuity to support Beit Avi Chai, a cultural center in the heart of Jerusalem, the pressure to exhaust all funds wasn't present. "Our goal is to do everything as smartly as we can with the spend-down, and if we end up leaving a larger amount than planned, this will increase the funds available for Beit Avi Chai," says Yossi Prager, executive director. But sunsetting did push Avi Chai to think strategically about how best to help other grantees for whom the foundation tended to be the sole or primary funder. Avi Chai has reached out to partners to help grantees maintain their programs into the future, has helped recipients improve their fundraising capacities, and has encouraged grantees to plan for the future and merge with other nonprofits in some cases.

> Having the bulk of your charitable giving take place in your lifetime gives you direct oversight, and leaves behind an imprint to guide future disbursements.

Several decisions Zalman Bernstein made have protected his donor intent, according to Prager. Nearly all trustees knew Bernstein personally and worked with him on the board. Bernstein avoided naming professional grantmakers or family members other than his widow as trustees. Instead he chose individuals who were philosophically aligned with him. "That doesn't mean everybody always saw eye-to-eye—Israeli culture is different than American culture, and people on the other side of the ocean often had trouble seeing things the way people on this side of the ocean did—but the trustees agreed at the level of principles and purposes," Prager explains. "That pretty much guaranteed the foundation wasn't going to shift course." Second, Bernstein vested his trustees with genuine decisionmaking authority during his lifetime, while maintaining veto control. He never found it necessary to use his veto. Following his death, the trustees were already accustomed to leading—and equally accustomed to adhering to their founder's intent.

Prager believes that donors are wise to consider sunsetting, first to avoid mission drift in the future, but also because "you don't want perpetuity to stand in the way of seizing opportunities when they come." A spend-down can "encourage future trustees to seize the opportunity when it's available." At the same time, he cautions, the time pressure can compel significant spending even if there are not yet optimal giving opportunities within the foundation's funding areas.

Earhart Foundation is another example of a board of trustees deciding to sunset after the original wealth creator's death. Harry Earhart was born in 1870, one of eleven children. Son of a respected local businessman, he was also a cousin of pilot Amelia Earhart. He started several businesses, with his greatest success coming as a manufacturer of lubricating oils. Then he used his fortune to support some of the most influential thinkers of the twentieth century through his foundation.

After retiring in the early 1930s and settling in Ann Arbor, Michigan, he focused on various charitable and religious causes, initially through a family foundation. Over time, Earhart became concerned about threats to free enterprise and traditional values, concerns that his children did not share. In the early 1950s, he made the bold decision to remove his children from governance of the foundation, and constituted a new board comprised of businessmen who shared his philosophical outlook. It is one of the first known instances in which a donor reorganized his board to ensure future compliance with his intent.

Earhart passed away in 1954, leaving his foundation in the hands of the board. Although the foundation was established in perpetuity at this point, Earhart gave his trustees broad latitude in the bylaws to make a sunsetting decision at a later date. And although he left no formal guidance on focus areas for the foundation, trustees had a wealth of information from his correspondence: he was keen to create a better understanding of American founding principles, develop human talents, and strengthen the humanities and disciplines such as history, law, philosophy, and economics. In its subsequent grantmaking, Earhart Foundation exhibited a peerless knack for identifying talented, influential scholars. Nine winners of the Nobel Prize in economics were Earhart Fellows earlier in their careers, among them both Friedrich Hayek and Milton Friedman.

By the early 2000s, the foundation's leadership was beginning to weigh the question of sunsetting. David Kennedy—one of Earhart's grandchildren and the president of the foundation at the time—led the board of trustees through an exploration of where the foundation stood, and where it might go in the future. Concerned about the many historical violations of donor-intent violation, the board in

2005 opted for a ten-year sunsetting schedule, closing the foundation's doors in 2015. "While there was no particular threat to donor intent at the time, the board thought it prudent—given the age of the foundation and the longevity of its operations—that operating for another 10 years would give maximum guarantee that donor intent would continue to be observed faithfully," says former president Ingrid Gregg.

To ease the spend-down process, the Earhart board took several steps. It kept its grant portfolio largely unchanged—remaining committed to current grantees—while slightly increasing spending across the board. It also identified ten top-performing grantees and targeted them for special closure grants. "The goal was to avoid peaks and troughs of spending, but have a gradual increase in targeted areas," Gregg says. To ensure program consistency, the board was also careful to maintain existing staff throughout the closure process by instituting incentives (including financial ones) to encourage crucial managers to stay to the end. Communication with grantees was also paramount. "We really wanted to be transparent with our grantees because we were mindful of what it would mean for them to not have Earhart's resources available to them anymore."

In 2015, after more than seven decades in existence, Earhart Foundation officially went out of business. "Sunsetting can be a nimble and flexible process," concludes Gregg. "It can be tailored specifically to small family foundations or much larger foundations. While some donors might find the process a little intimidating, they should realize they don't have to be boxed into strategies or limited in their effectiveness."

A final word on sunsetting

In addition to the negative concerns that may lead you to opt for giving while living or limited-life philanthropy, there are positive reasons to avoid locking up your funds for future use. In America there is good reason to be optimistic about the wealth of coming generations, and the generosity of our next cohort of citizens. It makes more sense to spend now to solve your own problems rather than save money for future residents who will likely have more options anyway due to their greater affluence. The best boost you can give to the future is to fix the now.

Julius Rosenwald understood this intuitively. He decided to have his foundation sunset not only to maximize his effect on the vital needs of his day, but also because he recognized that "Coming generations can be relied

Model donor—
John M. Olin Foundation

Perhaps the most referenced example of a philanthropy successfully sunsetting is the John M. Olin Foundation. This foundation exercised outsized influence in advancing conservative ideas in the last quarter of the twentieth century, having made a deliberate decision to concentrate its efforts during a compact period of time, instead of holding back financial resources for years into the future. Although the foundation's assets never totaled more than $150 million, its spending during the 1980s and 1990s exceeded that of many larger foundations.

Born in 1892 in Alton, Illinois, John Olin was the son of a businessman who owned a gunpowder mill. After majoring in chemistry at Cornell University he joined the family business, which had grown into the Western Cartridge Company. His product development and management skills spurred significant growth, and when the Second World War erupted, his family firm—rechristened Olin Industries—became a major supplier of ammunition to U.S. and Allied forces. After the war, the company expanded into chemical production and other areas. By the early 1950s Olin was a very wealthy man.

The John M. Olin Foundation was founded in 1953. For several years, it functioned like many perpetual foundations, making annual grants to Olin's alma mater and other causes. Alert to Vietnam-era disturbances on many campuses, including Cornell University, Olin shifted his focus in the early 1970s to the defense of free enterprise and limited government. "I would like to use this fortune to help preserve the system which made its accumulation possible in only two lifetimes, my father's and mine," he said. To lead this endeavor, Olin recruited like-minded board members and appointed former U.S. Treasury Secretary William Simon as foundation president.

Rosenwald's example, coupled with Henry Ford II's resignation from the Ford Foundation in 1976, prompted Olin to make another crucial decision: to sunset his foundation within 25 years of his death. Protecting donor intent was one factor, as was Olin's fear of increased government regulation of private foundations following the 1968 Tax Act. Another was Olin's desire to use his funds in concentrated doses to achieve high-yield results in a short period of time. The foundation's rapid spending, focused mission, and programmatic ingenuity allowed it to have an oversized impact during its time. During the late 1980s and early 1990s, the Olin Foundation spent $20 million per year, while a typical foundation of Olin's size operating in perpetuity would have capped its annual spending at about a third of that.

A remarkable bull run in stocks between 1982 and 2000 extended Olin's reach. "We were able to turn out 12 to 18 percent returns consistently, so that helped us spend a lot and keep going," former president Jim Piereson notes. And America's intellectual climate between the late 1970s and the foundation's close in 2005 also presented a unique opportunity to create and fund organizations and individuals who were able to advance conservative intellectual life. Plus Olin Foundation leaders were unusually savvy in identifying individuals and groups with potential to influence social trends. Grantees included Allan Bloom, Milton Friedman, the American Enterprise Institute, Federalist Society, Heritage Foundation, Hoover Institution, and Manhattan Institute, and academic centers at major American universities that fostered conservative thought, including law-and-economics centers at prominent law schools. Experienced foundation observers—regardless of their personal politics—recognize Olin's accomplishments. In his 2017 book, *Putting Wealth to Work*, Duke University professor Joel Fleishman calls Olin "a textbook example of the potential of philanthropy to achieve significant results."

upon to provide for their own needs as they arise.... Wisdom, kindness of heart, and good will are not going to die with this generation."

Donors who choose this route must nonetheless deal with some thorny decisions. What timeframe is optimal for a sunset? How do you navigate the off-ramp so as to achieve objectives and avoid leaving programs hanging? How can your foundation best communicate with and support grantees who will lose funding after the sunset date? How can you retain crucial employees in your organization long enough to get the job done without doing serious damage to their future professional prospects? How best to handle the closure process itself (archiving materials and legal documents, disbursing residual assets, etc.)? There is no one-size-fits-all answer to these questions, but limited-life foundations are beginning to communicate more with each other and with the larger philanthropic community about "lessons learned" in the sunsetting process.

Meanwhile, sunsetting presents the strongest defenses for donor intent. As Frances Sykes puts it, "If you want to make an impact, spend down. If you are concerned about your foundation being a burden, or concerned about controlling your philanthropy from the grave, spend down. If you are concerned about funds being spent on family retreats instead of going to grantees, spend down. If you are concerned about donor intent, spend down."

Creating a perpetual entity

The third option for grantmaking activity is to establish a philanthropic vehicle that will survive you—with no end date in mind. Open-ended timeframes carry several advantages. If your primary goal is long-term support for clearly specified geographic regions, issues, or institutions, then a perpetual grantmaking entity can be an attractive choice.

The problem of anticipating future needs is not insuperable, notes Linda Childears of the perpetual Daniels Fund: "If you pick things like our donor Bill Daniels did—aging, early childhood, K-12 education—those are not ever going to be solved or go away." And Daniels' geographic focus on the states where he earned his fortune will likewise never become out of date or problematic. In addition, Joel Fleishman points out that perpetual foundations have made possible "the birth and nurturing" of many major national charities built over decades of support.

Nor is it impossible for a foundation to operate over a long term while protecting donor intent, as some examples in this guidebook demonstrate. Attention to your governing documents and structures becomes even more critical for those foundations with no defined end date, though. What happens when those elements are deficient?

Codifying donor intent after the donor's death

The Foellinger Foundation of Fort Wayne, Indiana, was created in 1958 by Helene Foellinger and her mother Ester. Helene was publisher at the *News-Sentinel* from 1936 to 1980, one of the few female newspaper publishers at the time and certainly one of the youngest. Helene specifically wanted her foundation to operate in perpetuity, so even though the board discussed sunsetting a few years ago, it ultimately decided to continue with no end date.

The Foellingers' philanthropic interests were strictly geographic. All grants were to support causes in Allen County, Indiana, with nine out of ten going to early childhood, youth, and family-development efforts, particularly for those who are most in need. Following Helene's death in 1987 and the settlement of her estate, the foundation's assets jumped from $20 million to $70 million.

The first key to protecting donor intent at the Foellinger Foundation after Helene passed away was putting the right person in charge. Helene trusted Carl Rolfsen and indicated in writing that he should head the foundation. "For many years, he was the voice of donor intent," says Cheryl Taylor, president of the foundation from 2001 to 2020.

By 2000 Rolfsen and the board began to realize the need to document more formally the founders' vision for future generations, but neither Helene nor Ester had left a written mission statement or detailed statement of intent. To document the Foellingers' goals, Rolfsen and his board found speeches that Helene had given on personal responsibility. Those "very much highlighted her personal philosophy," says Taylor, "in articulating the difference between the individual's role and the community's role." Remarkably, the Foellinger Foundation halted grantmaking during a two-year period between 2000 and 2002 to focus exclusively on codifying its founders' vision.

Rolfsen also turned his attention to the selection of future board members. He and his colleagues developed an exhaustive approach to board recruitment. Board nominees must come through a committee structure, and each new board member is assigned a mentor (an experienced board member). Upon arrival, the new members receive an intensive course in the Foellingers' intent, and each is required to sign a statement affirming that intent.

The Harry and Jeanette Weinberg Foundation, based just outside Baltimore, made a similar transition. After his family immigrated to the U.S. from Eastern Europe in the early twentieth century, Harry Weinberg quickly showed a propensity for business. He left home as a teenager to make his way, and throughout the 1950s and 1960s built a diverse transportation empire, and accumulated wealth in securities and real estate. With a keen philanthropic heart—as early as the 1930s Harry Weinberg was helping Jews escape Germany and find safe haven in the U.S.—he created the Weinberg Foundation to aid the poor and vulnerable, with a special emphasis on Jews.

Harry Weinberg passed away in 1990. The foundation's charter has always specified a desire to help people in the lower half of the economic spectrum, but with a few exceptions delves into little detail beyond that. It was incumbent upon the first generation of trustees to take what they knew about Harry's philanthropic aspirations and apply them faithfully. They based their understanding of his donor intent both on Harry's writings and on his spoken words.

By 2005, with a new president and some new trustees, it was time to codify Harry's donor intent formally, and more clearly identify the geographic and issue areas where grants would be made. "We were looking at what Harry would have wanted, and what would be consistent with his goal of helping poor people," says Donn Weinberg, Harry's nephew and a trustee of the foundation through 2018. The trustees settled on particular programs supporting jobs, housing, health, and education, with a special emphasis on the elderly, at-risk children, and veterans. Grantmaking is also directed at rural communities in the United States, and Israel. Today, the foundation that Harry Weinberg founded in 1959 has assets totaling $2.6 billion, and continues to fund programs that provide services and create opportunity for vulnerable populations.

If you are determined to create a foundation designed to last in perpetuity, and you want to prevent—or at least limit—the erosion of donor intent, then you should consider the following steps (which are discussed further in other chapters).

- Incorporate carefully worded mission statements and other donor-intent documents into your foundation's articles of incorporation and bylaws and require a significant board majority vote to alter those documents. For example, the Hilton Foundation added the following clause to its articles of incorporation in 2014: "The corporation shall make distributions and conduct activities in accordance with the philosophy of Conrad N. Hilton, which philosophy includes religious, ethical, business, and conservative beliefs." Make supplementary materials like oral histories and videos of the donor available to trustees, as well.
- If such documents are not available, follow the example of the Foellinger and Weinberg foundations and create a contemporary donor-intent statement based on personal knowledge of the donor and on letters, speeches, or other writings that provide insight into the donor's values, principles, and key interests.
- Implement the requirement used at the Daniels Fund, Foellinger Foundation, and other places that trustees sign a statement

acknowledging the donor's intent and their commitment to honor it. See chapter 8.

- Have the donor-intent statement read out loud at least once a year at a board meeting, as the Duke Endowment does.
- Follow the Templeton Foundation practice of scheduling regular independent donor-intent audits of your grantmaking.
- Give outside parties legal standing to take action against your board if it strays from its mission.

Of course, none of these practices are foolproof: If future trustees are intent on upending your donor intent, they will most likely be able to do so. When all is said and done, no matter how clearly you define your intentions in writing, no matter how judiciously you populate your board of trustees with trusted colleagues, there is no firm legal barrier to significant drift in the mission of your perpetual foundation. Future trustees and staff may steer your foundation away from your intent as memory of your life fades.

"Western law has done away with ancestor worship. No legally enforceable duties exist to the dead," state philanthropy experts Fred Fransen and Keith Whitaker in their article "Preserving Donor Intent." "As currently constituted, foundations, in effect, have no accountability mechanism, save in the case of egregious violations of the law that come to the attention of their state's attorney general," adds Heather Higgins, president and director of the Randolph Foundation in New York City. In the Philanthropy Roundtable publication *Should Foundations Exist in Perpetuity?* she warns that "No one really referees the actions of foundation trustees, and no forces visit negative consequences upon them when they make poor decisions. Their latitude is extraordinary because the work they do is presumed to be for the public good."

Recent critics of philanthropy actually encourage the dismissal of donor intent. In his 2018 book, *Just Giving: Why Philanthropy is Failing Democracy and How It Can Do Better*, Stanford University professor Rob Reich maintains that "the foundation is defensible only when philanthropic assets are directed for long-term social experimentation," and so "the state must always retain the right to intervene in a philanthropic endowment." Reich wields quotes from John Stuart Mill to argue that a "dead man's intentions for a single day" should not be allowed to morph into a "rule for subsequent centuries."

Even less ideological observers see pitfalls in perpetual foundations. Rosenwald was one of the first philanthropists to caution his

Model donor—Lynde and Harry Bradley Foundation

Lynde and Harry Bradley were brothers and business partners who led a manufacturing business, the Allen-Bradley Company of Milwaukee, Wisconsin. Founded in 1903, the company experienced significant growth during World War I due to the Allies' need for naval electrical equipment, artillery firing mechanisms, and radio apparatus. By the war's end, Allen-Bradley had expanded to fill nearly a city block. By the 1960s, it had become one of the largest manufacturing concerns of its type in the country.

With six years separating them, the brothers were never close confidants, but their dramatically different personalities enabled them to establish a partnership that guided Allen-Bradley through its growth years. Lynde was quiet, retiring, and austere, a man who preferred to tinker in his labs and workrooms, handling research and development of new products. Harry was gregarious and focused on sales and personnel management.

The Bradley brothers were kind and generous to their workers, creating a workplace that provided extensive amenities: a wood-paneled reading room, a sundeck, on-site medical care, and a company jazz orchestra. They resisted unionization, and both brothers (particularly Harry) had strong conservative beliefs which later shaped their philanthropic giving.

After a brief illness, Lynde passed away in 1942. Most of his shares in the company were poured into a series of interlocking trusts that kept management of the company intact while providing income to Harry and other family members. Close to the time of his death, Lynde had been working to establish a foundation, and Harry partnered with Lynde's wife, Caroline, to complete the process. Initial giving was focused on Milwaukee nonprofits and schools.

Harry Bradley's philanthropy soon turned to public-policy causes. He was deeply anti-communist, a supporter of Robert Taft for President in 1952, and a major backer of Barry Goldwater in 1964. He supported the Hoover Institution and conservative radio programs in the Midwest. And he provided early and frequent support to William F. Buckley Jr.'s *National Review* to help the magazine through its financially rocky years. Harry passed away in 1965.

In the 1960s and 1970s, public-policy grants became even more frequent. The Bradley Foundation supported groups such as the Intercollegiate Studies Institute and Morality in Media. Even so, most giving went to local organizations like Marquette Medical School and St. Luke's Hospital.

In 1985, the Allen-Bradley company was purchased for $1.7 billion. The foundation started by the brothers ballooned overnight from $14 million to almost $300 million in assets. The Bradley Foundation now grants between $35 and $45 million annually to hundreds of charities in Milwaukee and conservative causes across the U.S. Since 1985, the foundation has made more than 13,000 grants totaling over $1 billion to more than 1,900 organizations.

Bradley is one example of a foundation operating in perpetuity that has preserved donor intent, even though many decades now separate the foundation's work and Lynde and Harry Bradley's original philanthropic giving. "We spend an enormous amount of time—both staff and board—reflecting on what Lynde and Harry would have done today had they still been here," says president Richard Graber.

With that commitment in mind, board and staff recently underwent a planning process that yielded four focus areas: Constitutional order, free markets, civil society, and informed citizens. While specific grantmaking targets may change over time, the foundation adheres to the values and principles of its donors: "Lynde and Harry Bradley believed not just in freedom, but also in the richness of community and culture that are the basis of a well-lived life. The Bradley Foundation seeks to further those beliefs by supporting the study, defense, and practice of the individual initiative and ordered liberty that lead to prosperity, strong families, and vibrant communities."

To Graber, there are two ingredients in the Bradley Foundation's long-term fidelity to donor intent. First, have a rigorous process for selecting new board members and staff that ensures they are philosophically compatible. Second, thoroughly evaluate grant requests. "If you get these two things right—the people part, and the rigorous process for grantmaking—then you've got a pretty good chance of staying true to donor intent," says Graber.

peers that "storing a large sum of money for long periods of time" resulted in "tendencies toward bureaucracy and a formal or perfunctory attitude toward the work." Similarly, Jeff Raikes warns about the propensity for perpetual foundations to play it safe in their philanthropic investments rather than take on bold projects. Foundations may be formed by entrepreneurs quite willing to take risks to solve problems, he notes, but "when you get into the third and fourth generation, the foundation ends up being more controlled by a set of trustees that may not have that willingness." In addition to having different temperaments, they have different incentives. Some trustees believe their foremost responsibility is "to protect the reputation of the institution. If they're trying to protect the reputation of the institution, will they feel empowered to take the risks that might lead to some significant failure? I think not."

"Whether it's decades from now or centuries from now, almost any purpose that you can think of will ultimately become obsolete or unfeasible, at which point whatever money is left—which could be quite a lot—is going to be used for another purpose, a purpose that you probably can't even conceive of, decided by people that you can't even imagine," warns Tom Riley. "If you're choosing perpetuity, then you are choosing that ultimately it will wind up going forward as something unfamiliar, run by people you don't know." As Jerry Hume of the Jaquelin Hume Foundation bluntly puts it, "You can't protect donor intent from the grave."

Donor intent in family foundations: A unique challenge

Establishing family foundations in perpetuity is a popular choice among donors. A recent survey by the National Center for Family Philanthropy found that 30 percent of the responding family foundations have opted for perpetuity, compared to just 10 percent who are spending down. (The remaining foundations are either undecided or plan to revisit the question periodically.) Another survey by Foundation Center concluded that two out of three family foundations plan to operate indefinitely. Frequently, perpetuity is an almost automatic choice for family foundations, based on a vision of a harmonious family legacy extending across multiple generations.

Multi-generation family philanthropy can be a source of great satisfaction, but donors who establish foundations, donor-advised funds, or other philanthropic vehicles for their families must first understand their own intentions and communicate them in clear terms to their family members, to their estate planners, and to their legal advisers. If you seek an opportunity for your family to come together and experience the joy of giving with few or no restrictions on mission, then engage your children in your charitable endeavors early and give them free rein.

John D. Rockefeller's personal giving was driven by his Baptist faith and his belief in a free-market economy. His family—now entering its seventh generation of philanthropy—has never been bound by any specific directive other than the notion that great wealth brings with it great responsibility. Successive generations of the family have shifted their giving priorities dramatically and experimented with a variety of grantmaking styles, heavily influenced by personal life experiences. The Rockefeller name, however, still binds them.

The Sobrato Family Foundation is a perpetual foundation based in California. Real-estate developer John Sobrato built many of the commercial structures in Silicon Valley. He and his wife, Susan, are

> Donors who establish family foundations with a vision of a harmonious family legacy nonetheless need to communicate their intentions in clear terms to family members.

the original wealth creators of Sobrato Philanthropies, an umbrella entity that includes their family foundation. The Sobratos have three children plus seven grandchildren, and all three generations are represented on the foundation's board of directors. Grandchildren are permitted to attend board meetings, and they may vote on grants after their 21st birthday. That's one step the Sobratos have taken to involve future generations in giving: exposing them to the process early on.

The family foundation has a specific mission: to make Silicon Valley a place of opportunity for all its residents by promoting access to high-quality education, career pathways, and essential human services. In addition to the main foundation, John and Susan have also allowed family members to pursue their individual charitable interests by creating donor-advised funds for them. When the Sobratos donate appreciated real estate to their foundation, they deposit half of the proceeds into these donor-advised funds, from which the children and grandchildren are free to make distributions without seeking board approval. "We hope that by doing this we encourage the family to continue giving together rather than drifting apart," John Sobrato told *Philanthropy* magazine in 2018. "Our giving keeps us close. Making decisions on our shared priorities creates a natural process for learning each other's passions and opinions."

In line with the family ethic of generosity, John and Susan Sobrato are also stewarding trust funds for their grandchildren. Sobrato heirs begin receiving distributions from their trusts at age 25, with incremental increases in payouts at intervals until age 50. But the twist is that in order to receive funds, each family member must donate an equal amount to charity—dollar for dollar. "We thought it was important to encourage our grandchildren and children to do as we do," John Sobrato says. "There's enough wealth that they're comfortable, but not to excess. And our kids aren't selfish, so they're okay with this."

There are other models for philanthropists who seek to encourage productive giving across multiple generations of a family foundation. Heirs involved with the Hilton and JM Foundations, respectively, have honored the original donors' wishes over many decades. Families strongly interlaced by religious faith appear to be especially able to act in comity across succeeding generations.

The Utah-based GFC Foundation (an acronym for God, Family, and Country) has transmitted its donor intent across three generations with a common denominator of faith as a key ingredient—in this case, the Church of Jesus Christ of Latter-day Saints. Although it was several decades before the family created an official mission statement for the foundation, core values were nonetheless passed from one generation to the next. Dudley Swim, a successful investment manager during the Great Depression, launched the foundation in 1941. He passed away in 1972, but his son and daughter-in-law, Gaylord and Laurie Swim, took up the mantle of the family's philanthropy. In 1994, Gaylord established the current version of the foundation. Beyond its grantmaking to numerous charities, the GFC Foundation has chartered a public-policy organization, the Sutherland Institute, and a local faith-based private school, American Heritage. The foundation now focuses on freedom, cultural renewal, K-12 education, higher education, and poverty relief.

Following Gaylord Swim's death in 2005, his son Stan Swim became a third-generation president of the foundation until July

2018. He credits his close-knit family for transmitting core values. "The way we were brought up is one of the most important preservatives of donor intent," he says. "If we have succeeded in perpetuating Dudley's values into the third generation, it is not because of anything written into our organizing documents or bylaws, which are boilerplate. Our determination to stay consistent comes from parental teaching, which for each generation has started in childhood. Family experiences, conversations, and educational choices have all played a role. Today we have spirited arguments over practical means but remain unified on principle."

Swim adds that the inculcation of gratitude and a stewardship responsibility is fundamental to keep the foundation "still reflecting my grandparents' and parents' priorities. And I think gratitude will do more to keep you on track than documents or papers. Gratitude is what makes those documents come to life." For nearly 80 years the family's shared faith and values across generations have served as a strong defense against the threat of straying from donor intent.

When money and family collide
Even with careful planning, donors should recognize that money, even money dedicated to charitable purposes, can be an enormously

Tips for involving family while protecting donor intent

Communicate your priorities to your children and grandchildren early and often.
Toby Neugebauer, co-founder of Texas-based Quantum Energy Partners, took his family on a 110-day worldwide trip to expose them to the slums of Mumbai, the orphanages of China, and the dirt-path villages of Tanzania—all toward the goal of ensuring that his sons develop a sense of the possibilities for responding to real need in the world with the money they will inherit.

Reinforce these early lessons with lasting documents that enhance your family's understanding of your intent.
Oral histories, videos, anything that can be pulled out later for study, will help cement what you say in person.

Have hard discussions around core values and pay attention to deep-seated differences.
Family members who disagree with your stated mission are not likely to change their minds, and many donors realize too late that forced togetherness around a foundation's board table can do irreparable harm to a family in its private life, rather than knitting its members together.

Be clear with family members that formal participation in your family philanthropy is voluntary, not obligatory.
Your children may simply not share your interest in charity, especially when they are beginning their professional lives and starting their own families.

Treat participation as a privilege that must be earned, not an automatic consequence of one's DNA.
Be clear from the beginning about who is eligible to help run the philanthropy, and the qualifications needed for board service. Avoid having it interpreted as a guaranteed right. Some children might be more appropriate than others. Will you include spouses or domestic partners? Stepchildren? Think those decisions through up front.

Consider a system of rotating board membership.
If the pool of potential family board members is large, or if you want to restrict the number of family members sitting on the board at any one time, something like three-year terms can helpful. After rotations, you might want to appoint particularly effective participants to longer service.

Consider appointing family members to an advisory board.
The governing board may not be the appropriate place for relatives. There are other places to participate, like bodies that generate ideas and offer expertise, without exerting control.

Consider even less formal alternatives to board membership.
You can engage family members in philanthropy without handing them

governance control. Consider temporary committees, prize boards, short-term investigations, publicity duties, gala chairmanships, etc.

Give family members limited discretionary grant privileges within your primary foundation.
This can allow them to pursue their own interests, without giving them a board seat. This can be a good choice for a family that is geographically dispersed. Discretionary grant allotments should never be so large that they distract from a foundation's core mission and instead create individual "fiefdoms" within the family; nor should they be used for grants which directly counter donor intent.

Create a separate foundation or a donor-advised fund where there is unity.
It can focus on causes and organizations where there is agreement and interest among family members.

Create a separate foundation or a donor-advised fund when there is division.
If family members disagree with—or are simply less interested in—your mission, you might want to provide them independently with smaller amounts of money to support charities of their own choosing.

Establish different foundations for each of your children.
The late Gerry Lenfest was wary of family foundations (which he called "generally a big mistake") and chose to limit the life of his foundation. He also wanted to involve his children in philanthropy, however, so when Lenfest and his wife sold their company they had each child set up his or her own foundation. This gave the Lenfest heirs an opportunity to pursue their personal charitable interests, while keeping the larger Lenfest Foundation focused on Gerry's goals of improving education and work for the young of Philadelphia.

Don't allow the foundation to become the only—or even the primary—vehicle for family interaction.
This is especially important when only some family members serve on the foundation board. Continue to convene the full family for private occasions completely apart from the activities of the foundation.

destructive force within families. Many founders fail to foresee that disbursing the family's philanthropic assets can become a contentious process, one that is often complicated with the introduction of multiple marriages, half-siblings, and so forth. It is very easy to overestimate feelings of familial fidelity and ancestral deference when members become dispersed by generations, locations, and experiences.

As Paul Schervish, director of the Boston College Center on Wealth and Philanthropy, puts it, "Affluence and wealth are like electricity. They can light up your house—or burn it down." Even apart from the many cases where tart philosophical differences grow up within a family, Al Mueller of Excellence in Giving warns, "people give away somebody else's money differently than they give away money they had a part in making." Second- and third-generation philanthropy can take a toll on even the strongest clan.

A recent and well-publicized family feud centered on philanthropy involves the Surdna Foundation, one of the larger charities in the U.S., with $1 billion in assets. Surdna is over 100 years old, and 380 living adult descendants of the founder are kept abreast of the foundation's work through regular e-mails and reports. In May 2018 almost two dozen of these descendants signed a letter to the board decrying an exaggerated focus on social-justice causes which they say the foundation's creator, John Andrus—an investor and businessman in pharmaceuticals, real estate, railroads, and utilities—would have found objectionable. The dissenting family members particularly balked at the pending hire of a new foundation president with close ties to progressive politics.

Until his death in 1934, Andrus's charitable donations went to mainstay institutions like hospitals, schools, churches, and orphanages. Unfortunately, he left behind no statement explaining his donor intent, no instructions on board membership and succession, and no mission details beyond the boilerplate "religious, charitable, scientific, educational and eleemosynary purposes...." Perhaps he assumed his family would follow the clues he left behind in his own giving. Perhaps he intended for them to have complete flexibility. What seems certain is that he did not intend to launch a bitter—and public—family dispute eight decades after his death.

Kim Dennis of the Searle Freedom Trust cautions that family foundations are most problematic if your central purpose in giving is philosophical or ideological. "Family members do feel more of a claim to the money than non-family members do, so I think donors should weigh what matters more to them. Often, they want to blend the family and the purpose, and that's very hard to do. It can work—it has in our case—but if you really care about the mission, don't expect to be able to include your family members and have that succeed."

"A donor might create a family foundation expecting to unify family members," Dennis continues. "But money is a divisive thing. It's more likely to create conflict within a family than to bring everyone together."

Frances Sykes chose to sunset her foundation partly to lighten the load for her heirs. "I don't want to burden my children with causes they might or might not believe in," she says. "Why should I burden them with trying to carry through my intent, which might not be their intent?"

The questionable track record of family foundations when it comes to donor intent has prompted many donors to approach family giving cautiously, or steer clear of it altogether. Regardless of precautions, sooner or later a family foundation that operates in perpetuity requires you to entrust your donor intent to future generations. "Donors need to be honest with themselves," advises philanthropic counselor Keith Whitaker. "Am I willing to let my family members do what they think is best at a future time? Or am I seeking to change the world in a particular way? If so, then I better do it while I'm living."

Finding the Right Vehicle
For Your Mission

The vehicle you choose for your philanthropy has significant bearing on whether your donor intent will be honored. Some choices are a better fit than others, depending on what you hope to achieve with your giving, what timeframe you select, and whether you intend to involve family in your philanthropy. The purpose of this chapter is to evaluate the various options available through the lens of donor intent.

The good news is that you're not limited to one choice; many donors utilize more than one charitable vehicle. In general, vehicles that give you more flexibility in the here and now pose challenges for donor intent in the future, and vice versa. This chapter explores the most popular approaches, including private non-operating foundations, charitable trusts, non-stock corporations, operating foundations, donor-advised funds, philanthropically driven limited-liability companies, community foundations, supporting organizations, and philanthropic partnerships.

Private non-operating foundations

Traditionally, most donors choose to create private non-operating foundations as the vehicle for their philanthropy. "Non-operating" simply means that your foundation's chief goal is to make grants to various nonprofit organizations and not run your own programs. Most of the very large and well-recognized foundations—Ford, Gates, Packard, Rockefeller—are structured this way. But so are tens of thousands of others, many of them very small.

Donors who establish private non-operating foundations may claim a charitable deduction for up to 30 percent of adjusted gross income (AGI) for cash donations and up to 20 percent of AGI for appreciated securities and other property, with a five-year carry-forward. Publicly traded stock may be valued at fair market value, while other types of property may be valued at cost only. These entities are required by federal law to make an annual distribution of at least 5 percent of assets, pay an excise tax on investment income, limit the percentage of business enterprises they own, avoid self-dealing and grants to partisan political organizations, and file a 990-PF tax return. Typically, a private foundation derives its endowment from a single source—from an original wealth creator, a family, or a corporation—and is managed by a board of trustees in compliance with state and federal laws in addition to the foundation's bylaws, trust agreement, or articles of incorporation.

Private non-operating foundations offer both benefits and drawbacks:

- *PRO: Flexibility, autonomy, and control*
  Private foundations offer you considerable leeway to operate and allocate your charitable dollars as you see fit, largely free from government interference outside of legal regulations and mandatory reporting. You define the mission of your foundation,

choose its lifespan, make investment decisions about its endowment, and hire staff to manage grants and financial matters.

- CON: *Malleability, impermanence*
That same latitude poses challenges. Depending on how you structure your foundation, future boards of trustees may amend its mission, bylaws, articles of incorporation, operations, leadership, and so forth in ways that counter your decisions.

- PRO: *The ability to create a family legacy*
If one of your chief goals is to create a philanthropic legacy for your family, a private non-operating foundation may be the right choice. This vehicle can extend your giving through future generations, involving children and grandchildren in governance and grantmaking. As explored in Chapter 3 and other previous material, though, family foundations also pose certain risks to family peace, and to donor intent.

> Charitable vehicles that give you
> more flexibility now pose challenges
> for donor intent in the future.

- CON: *Increased complexity and risk of bureaucratic bloat*
The IRS demands substantial reporting and paperwork from foundations, and some states, like California, also require annual audits. You will likely need help complying with state and federal regulations and filing appropriate reports. Hiring professional staff can pose challenges for donor intent, is costly, and requires human-resource management and compliance with employment laws. In larger private foundations, a complex staff structure can contribute to bureaucratic bloat.

If you decide to use a private non-operating foundation as your philanthropic vehicle, you have two structural options: a charitable trust or a not-for-profit corporation, both of which are treated similarly by the Internal Revenue Service. Each structure has advantages and disadvantages that bear directly on donor intent, so the appropriate one for you depends on your objectives, your tolerance for change, and your desire for flexibility.

Sub-option 1: Charitable trusts

A trust is frequently the better instrument to protect donor intent because its organizational structure and funding guidelines, once established, can be changed only by court order unless a donor permits them. In theory, the rigidity of the trust instrument provides an added buffer against donor-intent violations. If you establish a trust with clear philanthropic parameters, your future trustees will face an enormous challenge amending that document. Doing so would require legal action involving the attorney general in the state where your entity is established, and trustees would be required to convince both the attorney general and the court that the original purpose of the trust is either impossible or impracticable. In these cases, the courts may invoke the *cy pres* doctrine to devise a course of action that comes as close as possible to the trust's original charitable purpose. Courts and attorneys general may vary, of course, in how narrowly or broadly they interpret your intent.

But while a charitable trust structure generally offers the strongest shield against legally sanctioned breaches of donor intent, it is not a fail-safe mechanism. Within the last 50 years, serious violations of donor intent have occurred within charitable trusts when neither trustees nor grantees objected. Even if complaints are registered, you cannot guarantee that your state's attorney general will step in to defend donor intent. "In some cases, an attorney general will step in and do a great job, but in some they don't do much," observes Paul Rhoads, president of the Grover Hermann Foundation.

The struggles of the John E. and Sue M. Jackson Family Trust over the past decade demonstrate the potential for donor-intent violations in charitable trusts. John and Sue Jackson created their wealth through the Pittsburgh-Des Moines Steel Company, a steel fabricator established in 1892 that helped erect the Gateway Arch in St. Louis, the Peace Bridge from Buffalo to Canada, and the "forked" columns in the World Trade Center. In 1950, the Jacksons created a charitable trust, naming John's brother, William R. Jackson, and the Commonwealth Trust Company of Pittsburgh (later the National City Bank of Pennsylvania) as co-trustees with equal voting power. Currently, John and Sue's niece and nephew, Polly Townsend and Dick Jackson, are trustees with a combined 50 percent voting power, and PNC Bank is the successor corporate co-trustee after multiple bank mergers and acquisitions. From 1950 through 2006, annual grant decisions were family-driven, with the bank managing investments and ensuring legal compliance.

From the beginning, the trust instrument had provided that the trust would expire "three years after the date when its assets have been entirely deleted" and that there was "no limitation" on the amount of annual donations. The original grantors had made it possible for them or their successors to add funding to the trust or simply spend it out. In 2006, long after the donors had passed away, the two family trustees asked to terminate the trust, expressing their concerns that if the trust continued past their lifetimes, future trustees "will cause the trust assets to be distributed in a manner never contemplated by the grantors." PNC's predecessor, National City Bank, opposed the termination, and the court declined to terminate the Trust at that time.

In late 2008, PNC Financial acquired National City Bank and became the corporate trustee. Since then, the bank has made a number of changes with which the family trustees have disagreed: limiting grants to the IRS-mandated 5 percent minimum payout per year, unilaterally directing donations to Pittsburgh-area charities without consent of the family trustees, and rejecting grants to charities that support free-market and religious causes long supported by the Jackson Family Trust. In late November 2016, after years of disagreement over the proper role of donor intent, PNC filed an action in the Orphans' Court to resolve a deadlock over 2016 donations. The Orphans' Court ruled in PNC's favor without hearing any evidence regarding grantor intent.

The appeal to the Superior Court of Pennsylvania filed by the family trustees in early 2017 vacated the Orphans' Court's order and directed the lower court that evidence of donor intent and "the history of the trust's giving" were relevant, and that the trial court should consider whether the limited role of the bank co-trustee throughout the Trust's history means that the bank should defer to the family trustees on donation decisions. The Court rejected both PNC's exclusion of advocacy organizations and its insistence that preference be given to charities in Western Pennsylvania.

The Superior Court's striking recognition of donor intent as central to maintaining the integrity of the Jackson Family Trust requires the three trustees to work together to resolve their differences in a way that honors the original grantors' wishes. The hearing on donor intent recently concluded and a decision from the lower court is expected in 2020.

A trust vehicle, as the Jackson Family Trust example shows, cannot always prevent donor-intent violations, especially when the trust instrument includes vague grantmaking instructions and when future corporate co-trustees with significant voting authority fail to share or recognize the donor's values. But a careful and determined donor can increase the odds that a trust will stay true to its intended mission over time.

Henry Crowell, founder of Quaker Oats Company, established the Crowell Trust in 1927. Ninety years later, it still reflects Crowell's values and vision as a grantmaking organization whose $100 million endowment supports evangelical Christian organizations. Seeing other foundations drifting during his lifetime—and witnessing the secularization of his church denomination—Crowell gave great attention to protecting his donor intent.

He clearly defined his intent in writing, not only directing that the trust's resources be used to promote evangelical Christianity, but also explaining in detail the doctrines that underpin that movement. He structured his trust to be governed by five personal trustees and one corporate trustee and delineated their duties to ensure that the personal trustees would have sole responsibility for grant decisions and would also exercise oversight of the corporate trustee. He undertook a long and thorough vetting of his trustees, requiring them to submit in writing their own values and vision. His original trustees—a majority of whom were personally familiar with his philanthropy—would select their successors, taking care that each future trustee would be "an avowed disciple of Jesus Christ…who unreservedly believes in and subscribes in writing to the objects and purposes of this trust." At every annual meeting, trustees read aloud the indenture that Crowell wrote. And they evaluate grants to ensure that mission drift isn't occurring at recipient nonprofits.

If you choose a charitable trust as a philanthropic vehicle, here are some basic guidelines to protect donor intent:

- DO keep in mind that the same rigidity that may serve to protect your donor intent will also prevent you from amending the trust instrument without legal action. If you opt for a trust vehicle you are committed irrevocably to certain philanthropic goals.
- In choosing a financial institution to hold your trust, DON'T assume that the close relationships you currently enjoy for your personal or business banking will last through future management changes.
- DO make clear in writing your philanthropic intentions, clarifying your values, your charitable purpose, and your operating principles (including spending policy and timeframe).

- DO design a governance structure in which the trustees you select hold majority control and establish a succession process with criteria tied to your donor intent.
- DO work directly with your initial trustees for a period of time so that they better understand your values and principles and your preferred strategies for evaluating grantees.
- DON'T leave the mission of your trust to chance.
- DO avoid potential court challenges by specifying alternative funding options for objectives that may be impossible to pursue in the future.
- DO take the time to understand the charitable laws and judicial treatment of trusts in the state in which your trust will operate. They vary from one jurisdiction to another.

Sub-option 2: Not-for-profit corporations

A foundation created as a not-for-profit corporation offers greater flexibility than a charitable trust. Although the corporation form requires more paperwork and record-keeping than a trust, it makes some things easier, like the hiring of employees and the initiation of contracts. The flexibility of a corporation does, however, include serious drawbacks for donor intent. Your foundation's charter or bylaws may be amended more easily, sometimes by a simple majority vote of board members.

If your intention is to give future trustees *carte blanche* to use your charitable dollars as they see fit, this structure is fine. But if you are concerned about donor intent, then establishing a corporate structure for your foundation requires careful attention. Aside from time-limiting your foundation and creating a strong mission statement with supporting documentation (both discussed in previous chapters), you might consider a hybrid structure for your foundation. If permitted by your state's charity laws, a hybrid structure combines some advantages of both trusts and corporations. In this model, a donor can organize a foundation as a not-for-profit corporation with a board of directors, but provide that the corporation will have special "members" who are given the exclusive power to elect and remove members of the board or amend the articles of incorporation and bylaws. The donor could serve as the sole "member," or name someone who is specially trusted.

The Arthur M. Rupe Foundation in California and the T. W. Lewis Foundation in Arizona are two examples of foundations with hybrid "member" corporate structures. In the latter example, Thomas Lewis

Selecting a Jurisdiction for Charitable Trusts

Like the rules governing nonprofit corporations, the laws governing charitable trusts vary from state to state. The primary state law that governs the establishment of both private trusts and charitable trusts is the Uniform Trust Code, currently enacted (though in slightly differing versions) in 34 states and the District of Columbia. For states that have not enacted the Uniform Trust Code, each state has codified its own laws for trust creation, validity, modification, and termination.

A charitable trust is created when the donor executes a written instrument to empower and direct one or more trustees to administer and distribute the assets for charitable purposes. Although most states do not require registration of trusts with any court or other state office, there are some exceptions. Colorado, for example, requires the trustee of most trusts administered in the state to register the trust within 30 days of taking office. If the charitable trust is created under the will of a donor, the charitable trust may be automatically subject to ongoing court oversight.

A charitable trust is usually governed by the law of the jurisdiction chosen by the donor. Donors are generally granted broad discretion in this, with two primary exceptions. First, a charitable trust created by a will is initially governed by the law of the donor's domicile at the time of death. Second, choosing a particular state to govern the trust agreement will usually not be respected if the donor has no connection to that state. Donors who want to create trusts in states other than where they reside should appoint a trustee from that jurisdiction; many states will recognize this.

When creating a private trust, a donor should evaluate the advantages and disadvantages of state law by looking at a few key considerations including, for example: the income tax treatment of the trust, the ease and cost associated with hiring a resident trustee, any creditor protection afforded to the trust, whether the trust can continue in perpetuity or for some lesser period of time, the ability to later modify the trust, and whether trustees are required to provide information, accountings, and/or notices to the trust beneficiaries. States such as Delaware, Nevada, New

Hampshire, South Dakota, Tennessee, and Wyoming are among the favorite jurisdictions for trust practitioners for the reasons mentioned above.

However, some of the factors that may favor creating a *private* trust under a specific state's laws may not be relevant for establishing a *charitable* trust. For example, income taxation issues are generally not relevant to charitable trusts. In addition, charitable trusts can exist in perpetuity even in states that restrict the perpetuities period for private trusts.

In contrast to state nonprofit corporation law, state trust law has few default rules regarding the internal governance of a charitable trust (with the exception of the management of the trust's investible assets). For example, state nonprofit corporation statutes usually include rules related to number, qualification, and appointment of directors and officers, meetings, voting, and other internal governance matters. No such rules generally apply to trusts, so donors must carefully consider the pros and cons of greater flexibility. What works for a living donor, and the trustees whom he or she has personally selected, may well lead to turmoil after the settler's death, especially if clear succession and governance rules are not set forth in the trust terms. One option for charitable trusts is to include a "trust protector," who can be given the authority to remove and replace trustees—and/or other limited powers over the trust—depending on state law.

It is not permissible under any circumstances to amend the purposes of a charitable trust such that the purposes no longer qualify the trust as a charitable entity. However, the terms of a trust may permit modification of the trust's purposes (especially, for example, during the donor's lifetime) as long as the purposes remain charitable. When the trust instrument does not contain the express power to modify the purposes of a charitable trust, the trustees of the trust can petition the court to apply the doctrine of *cy pres* (which translates to "as near as") to modify or terminate the trust. State law prescribes the standards by which the court may modify or terminate a charitable trust, and historically, this standard has required demonstrating that the purposes of the charitable trust were impractical or impossible to carry out. Some states, such as Delaware, have restricted the application of *cy pres* so that the court may intervene to modify the charitable purposes of the trust only when the stated purposes have become unlawful. A more restrictive application of this doctrine means that donor intent is more likely to be preserved.

When selecting a jurisdiction for a charitable trust, donors should also consider enforcement. The state attorney general always has standing to enforce a charitable trust, and many states give the donor standing to enforce the trust terms as well. But state law is not uniform with respect to whether others have standing including, for example, the donor's heirs or personal representatives.

Finally, it is important to note that donor intent can be incorporated through the terms of the trust, but also by imposing restrictions on a charitable contribution. Thus, a donor may create a charitable trust with fairly flexible provisions but include more restrictive provisions when making certain contributions to the trust. Generally, the gift would be structured as conditioned on certain additional requirements or restrictions, and by accepting the gift, the charitable trust is contractually agreeing to these additional requirements or restrictions. In such circumstances, state trust law will generally apply to the restricted charitable gift. It is important to consult with advisers in structuring such a conditional gift to ensure that the gift restrictions are both permissible and effective.

himself is the sole member, and he appoints the seven board directors. Following the death of Lewis and his wife, the board will become three family members and four non-family members and will operate on a 10- to 20-year sunset schedule. Donors who are not time-limiting their foundations (family foundations intended to operate for many generations are a good example) may establish a trust to serve as the sole member of the corporation. The trust instrument should include a detailed statement of donor intent and the purposes of the corporation; specific criteria for trustees and a plan for trustee succession; and a clear prohibition against changing the original charitable mission of the foundation.

Private operating foundations

If you have a very specific philanthropic goal that few, if any, charities are fulfilling, an operating foundation could be your best choice. With this option your foundation funds its own charitable services and programs—meaning you will likely make only minimal grants to outside organizations. An operating foundation must spend at least 85 percent of its adjusted net income or its minimum investment return directly on its own activities. An operating foundation brings several distinct benefits.

It is exempt from minimum charitable distribution requirements. It provides tax deductions for cash contributions up to 60 percent of a donor's adjusted gross income (compared to the typical limitation of 30 percent for non-operating foundations). It may receive distributions from independent non-operating foundations and is not subject to the public support test.

Operating foundations are engaged in a wide variety of activities. Among the better-known operating foundations:

- J. Paul Getty Trust, which operates the J. Paul Getty Museum in Los Angeles and also supports a multi-faceted arts program that includes conservation, research, publications, and training.
- Casey Family Programs, which provides direct services and conducts research on child and family well-being.
- Open Society Institute, Baltimore, which runs programs in criminal justice, youth development, and health.
- Broad Art Foundation, which was created in 1984 to lend works from its 700-piece collection without charging fees, and serve as a study center for art professionals, collectors, and students.
- Henry J. Kaiser Family Foundation, which conducts health research.
- Carnegie Foundation for the Advancement of Teaching, which funds both research and programs promoting improvement in education.

Liberty Fund is an operating foundation created to nurture a distinct ideology. Its programs are intended "to enrich understanding and appreciation of the complex nature of a society of free and responsible individuals and to contribute to its preservation." Founded in 1960 by Pierre Goodrich, an Indianapolis businessman and attorney, Liberty Fund reflects its donor's deep interest in public affairs and his love for the Great Books.

Although it functioned as a grantmaking foundation in its early years, Liberty Fund converted to an operating foundation in 1979. Since then it has sponsored its own programs, including more than 3,000 conferences for scholars and students on topics such as "Liberty and Markets in the Writings of Adam Smith" and "Shakespeare's Conception of Political Liberty." Liberty Fund has also published over 400 titles in both print and e-books, most of them exploring "the interrelationship of liberty and responsibility in individual life, society, and governance." In addition to the conferences and books, Liberty Fund maintains a free online library of important writing on individual liberty, limited government, and free markets. Donors with missions as distinct and specific as that of Pierre Goodrich may well see a private operating foundation as their most effective vehicle for philanthropy.

In protecting donor intent, operating foundations have one obvious advantage. Because these organizations fund, design, and administer their own programs, they have direct control over how their funds are spent, side-stepping grantees who may fail to adhere to the terms of a grant agreement. But operating foundations are not foolproof. They are subject to many of the same problems as non-operating foundations, including wayward board or staff members and mission creep over time. While an operating foundation gives you more immediate control over how your charitable funds are directed, it cannot guarantee fidelity to your intent in perpetuity.

Philanthropic LLCs

If you seek maximum flexibility in your philanthropy, you might consider bypassing the tax-exempt route and forming a for-profit limited-liability company (LLC). The benefits of LLCs in charitable work are numerous: wider latitude and diversity of spending opportunities, less regulation and red tape, and augmented privacy and control.

Facebook founder Mark Zuckerberg and his wife Priscilla Chan chose this vehicle in 2015. Declaring their intention to donate 99 percent of their Facebook shares to charitable causes in their lifetimes (an estimated $45 billion pledge when it was made), they formed an LLC (the Chan Zuckerberg Initiative) to accompany the existing Chan Zuckerberg Foundation (a private non-operating foundation) and the sizeable donor-advised fund which the couple has funded at the Silicon Valley Community Foundation. Philanthropic LLCs are popular with other Silicon Valley powerbrokers as well, including Pierre Omidyar, Steven Ballmer, and Laurene Powell Jobs, widow of Apple founder Steve Jobs.

In early 2019, John and Laura Arnold announced the restructuring of their philanthropy as an LLC, Arnold Ventures, which overarches the Laura and John Arnold Foundation (a private foundation), the Arnolds' donor-advised fund, and their 501c4 Action Now Initiative. President Kelli Rhee explains that for philanthropic work on topics like criminal justice, health care, and school performance, an LLC structure fits the Arnolds' aims. Although grants to c3 nonprofit organizations will continue to come from the private foundation and donor-advised fund, "We realized that in order to create change that lasts, we would need to

Domicile considerations:
Where to incorporate?

Laws governing trusts and not-for-profit corporations vary from state to state. Choosing a home for your foundation can be important in protecting donor intent.

Delaware is generally the preferred jurisdiction for corporations, including nonprofit corporations, and is the legal home to many foundations that fund exclusively in other states. Delaware provides many advantages:

- The Delaware General Corporation Law (DGCL) is a modern, current, and internationally recognized and copied corporation statute that is updated frequently to take into account new business and court developments.
- Delaware offers a well-developed body of case law interpreting the DGCL which offers certainty in planning.
- The Delaware Court of Chancery is considered by many to be the nation's leading business-entity court, where judges expert in corporate and governance matters deal with issues regularly and efficiently.
- Delaware offers a user-friendly Division of Corporation office for document filings.

Delaware governs its nonprofit corporations under the same state rules as for-profit corporations. The Delaware corporate law is considered very flexible, and is even more accommodating for non-stock corporations. There are provisions in the Delaware law which allow non-stock corporations to choose how to organize their internal governance, including placing restrictions on the power of the board.

A primary principle in Delaware corporate law is that the board of directors has the ultimate authority to manage and direct the affairs of the corporation. Most corporations find it desirable for the board to have such broad power to make substantial changes to the corporation over time. For nonprofit corporations, however, this means that even ultimate purposes and mission can be changed. To protect donor intent it may therefore be desirable to restrict the board's power over the corporation, particularly where a founding donor of a private foundation wishes to ensure that his or her foundation will continue to adhere to certain values, or support a particular giving area or geography, even if a distant future board might wish to deviate from that. In Delaware the corporate board's power can be modified in such a way, so long as those provisions are included in the certificate of incorporation. One might, for instance, require a supermajority of the board for any fundamental change of mission. Or require that some outside person or entity have special rights to approve certain changes. Or a provision could simply say that the purposes may never be amended.

The states of Florida, Tennessee, and Texas can be attractive because they have enacted provisions into law that support philanthropic freedom and that restrict the state from attempting to direct foundations' charitable missions or demanding personal information about foundation trustees, staff, and grantees. Other important questions of state law include the scope of trustee indemnification, and provisions permitting a foundation to move to a new jurisdiction, allowing it to take advantage of another state's laws. As a donor, you should work closely with your attorney to determine where to incorporate. In any case, a foundation's "home state" will generally require it to register with the state's charities bureau.

remove barriers between data and decisive action, working swiftly across the policy-change spectrum," says Rhee.

The most obvious downsides to LLCs are the loss of a tax deduction for any funds donated to the entity, and the fact that income generated by LLCs will not be tax exempt. But donors may still write off on their personal tax filings funds donated through their LLCs to charitable causes.

The advantages of LLCs over private foundations are significant:

- They are not subject to annual distribution requirements.
- They give donors the latitude to invest in domestic and foreign for-profit ventures. For example, Powell Jobs' Emerson Collective bought a majority stake in the *Atlantic* magazine in 2017. The Omidyar Network has invested in Flutterwave, an African payment processing company, which it believes will improve African standards of living while operating as a business.
- When program staff are employed by an LLC (rather than by a c3 entity), they can move seamlessly from c3 to c4 to for-profit work.

- Donors can use LLCs to fund ballot initiatives, direct lobbying, political campaigns, and individual candidates—expenditures which are prohibited for private foundations.
- Donors can use LLCs to support foreign charities without the requirement imposed on private foundations to determine that prospective foreign grantees are the equivalents of Section 501c3 public charities.
- In contrast to a private foundation's tax return, LLC filings do not have to be public.

The benefits of charitable LLCs are numerous: wider diversity of spending opportunities, less red tape, augmented control, and privacy.

- LLCs permit donors to dedicate valuable chunks of their enterprises to philanthropic purposes without endangering their ownership of their businesses. Zuckerberg, for example, would have been gradually forced to relinquish control of Facebook if he and Chan had donated stock to their foundation rather than to an LLC, because of federal tax law forbidding excess business holdings.
- Through an LLC, donors may make concentrated investments without running afoul of federal or state rules.
- LLCs are not subject to the "self-dealing" rules applied to private foundations, so donors can structure their operations and compensation plans in ways that integrate their philanthropy with their business. (Donors who are using both LLCs and non-profit philanthropic vehicles do need to be alert to those rules, however.)

Because LLCs are designed and governed by their donors, they can typically avoid the common threats to donor intent. Their managers are employees, not the independent directors of a foundation. And LLCs can be terminated, and their assets transferred, any time their donors wish. They are ideal vehicles for donors committed to spending down their financial resources in their lifetimes. LLCs cannot pass to subsequent generations without incurring estate taxes. Donors who choose to transfer assets from an LLC to a tax-exempt vehicle (such as a private foundation) should consider making that transfer at a time when they can still take an active role in the governance and grantmaking of the new entity, in order to put in place the recommended policies and procedures to protect donor intent.

Donor-advised funds

If you want to protect your charitable intent in the simplest way possible, you would be wise to consider donor-advised funds (DAFs). These funds originated within community foundations as a way for donors to create individual philanthropic accounts from which they could recommend grants to nonprofit organizations. Today, DAFs have become a wildly popular choice. The National Philanthropic Trust reported that in 2018, 728,563 individual DAF accounts held assets totaling just over $121.4 billion. During that year, donors used these funds to recommend $23.4 billion in grants to qualified charities.

DAFs now outnumber private foundations by more than five to one, and are continuing to grow at a much faster rate. In 2018, the largest grantmaker in the country was the Fidelity Charitable Gift Fund with $5.2 billion in donor-recommended grants. "Think of a donor-advised fund as your own private foundation," urges DonorsTrust president Lawson Bader. "You just don't have to deal with the administrative side of things. It's cheaper than a foundation, and you don't have to solicit proposals."

Donor-advised funds offer flexibility, simplicity, cost savings, and anonymity. These funds have relatively few rules and restrictions. Donors can take a tax deduction for their contribution in the year they make the deposit into their DAF, even if they do not make a grant recommendation from those funds in the same year. Gifts of cash are tax-deductible up to 60 percent of adjusted gross income, and many DAF sponsors that host your fund will also accept gifts such as securities, art, land, and business assets deductible at 30 percent of AGI. DAFs are subject neither to the excise tax nor the annual payout mandate imposed on private foundations. And contrary to some critiques, DAFs have high payout rates, collectively averaging about 20 percent a year—close to four times the payout rate of a typical foundation.

The cost of maintaining a donor-advised fund is considerably lower than the cost of operating and administering a private foundation, since the administrative burden of processing applications, philanthropic planning, and tax, legal, and accounting services is carried out by the sponsoring organization. Sponsors charge DAF holders an annual fee for these services, typically ranging from .5 to 1.5 percent of assets held in the fund.

Donor privacy is an especially important benefit of donor-advised funds. Although the sponsoring organization is required by law to disclose its grants, that disclosure does not include the name of the DAF account from which the gift originated. As the accountholder, you can choose whether your fund's name and your contact information are disclosed to the receiving charity. This is a critical factor for individuals who do not want to be inundated with solicitations or who simply want to keep their charitable giving confidential, and distinguishes DAFs from private foundations, which must list their grants in their annual tax filings. Some donors include both foundations and DAFs in their giving strategies, using DAFs to give family members latitude to make their own gifts, or to provide younger family members with a low-risk method of philanthropic "training," or to protect their privacy completely.

You may open a donor-advised fund through the sponsoring organization of your choice. If your goal is broad philanthropic giving, your best choice might be a national fund (Fidelity, Schwab, Vanguard, National Philanthropic Trust, etc.) that gives you the leeway to support most tax-exempt charities without geographic or ideological limits. If you have a specific geography in mind for your giving, then a better choice may be the community foundation that focuses on that area, and can provide you with the knowledge and experience of both staff and fellow donors—an especially important advantage if you do not reside in the region your DAF supports. You can open a DAF at most national funds and community foundations with a modest contribution.

Some universities also offer alumni and friends the opportunity to open a donor-advised fund that will be managed within the school's endowment. These sponsors, however, will typically impose a high minimum amount for distributions, and will also require that some percentage of the fund goes to the university. Yale University, for example, mandates that distributions be made in amounts of $50,000 or more, and that at least 50 percent of the funds contributed must eventually be allocated to Yale.

Protecting your donor intent with a donor-advised fund requires that you be mindful of the policies of the sponsoring organization. Because contributions to DAFs are irrevocable, it is critical that you understand that the sponsoring organization is the legal owner of the funds in your

DAF account, and that you merely "advise" on their use. Donor recommendations are typically accepted, but there have been exceptions. Sponsoring organizations have the option to reject donor recommendations to certain organizations, and some have responded to pressure from left-wing activists to shun subjectively labeled "hate groups" or other charities for ideological reasons. You should inquire about this practice in choosing a sponsoring organization for your DAF account.

If your philanthropy is oriented around a specific set of values—religious, philosophical, or ideological—then you may find that a mission-driven intermediary is the better sponsoring organization for your donor-advised fund account. Examples of such intermediaries include:

- National Christian Foundation
- Knights of Columbus Charitable Fund
- Jewish Federations of North America
- Tides Foundation
- DonorsTrust
- Bradley Impact Fund

Opening a DAF account at one of these organizations offers you the opportunity to engage in philanthropy with like-minded people. And because they share your philosophical values, these DAF sponsors are far more likely to serve as good stewards of your philanthropic legacy. Their guidelines are clear about the grants they will approve. For example, the National Christian Foundation is forthcoming with prospective donor advisers that staff will "only approve giver-recommended grants to organizations whose purposes and activities align with NCF's beliefs and values."

The policies of sponsoring organizations vary significantly, so pay attention to their rules and make decisions that uphold your philanthropic mission. For instance, at Fidelity Charitable, a donor can bequeath a DAF account to family members or other individuals who are then free to make their own grant recommendations. Or a donor can name one or more specific charities as beneficiaries of all remaining funds in an account. At DonorsTrust, each original donor has the option of appointing a successor to advise on the account, but any grant recommendations must align with the original donor's intent. Either the original or the new adviser may choose a sunset date for the account. If no date is selected, DonorsTrust will close out the account within 20 years of the death of the successor.

If you want your DAF account to continue to reflect your grant-making choices, then choose successors who understand that they will be stewards of your philanthropic legacy and whose values and interests align with yours. Discuss your grantmaking preferences with them to assess their willingness to make grant recommendations in line with your wishes. You may want to leave some suggestions in writing or by video, especially if you are planning a significant gift in the future.

One final note: Donor-advised funds have experienced such a rapid rise in popularity that they have attracted scrutiny from philanthropy critics and regulators. There now exist proposals like limiting the life of donor-advised funds to 10 years or less, requiring an annual payout of at least 5 percent, mandating disclosure of grant recipients, and so forth. Donors considering a DAF account should monitor potential regulatory shifts to ensure that donor-advised funds continue to be the right vehicle to protect their philanthropic intent.

Donor-advised funds outnumber foundations by five to one, and are growing fast.
And contrary to critics, their payout rates average four times that of foundations.

Community foundations

More than 800 community foundations operate in the United States, serving areas large and small. What all community foundations share is a long-term commitment to their place, through the pooling of resources from many donors into a permanent endowment. Including gifts from donor-advised funds, community-foundation grants totaled more than $10 billion in 2018.

You don't have to use a donor-advised fund to give through a community foundation, particularly if you have wide-ranging interests in a particular locality. But be aware that if you go with a non-DAF option and add your donations to the broad pool of money in the community foundation, it will be impossible for you to enforce any specific donor intent down the road.

- If you give to a general unrestricted fund, the foundation will respond to community needs and fund its own priorities as it judges best.
- If you give to a field-of-interest fund your money will go to one broad priority, like arts and culture, children and youth, environment, etc., with all details at the discretion of the community fund managers.
- If you establish a designated fund, that can support a specific purpose like annual scholarships or particular local charities.

> From a donor-intent perspective, it's wise to explore giving options at community foundations with a good deal of caution.

Remember that all gifts to community foundations, including those which establish donor-advised funds, are gifts that you no longer legally control. A governing or distribution board—intended to reflect community interests—typically oversees grantmaking, so your contribution could go to a cause you find objectionable. Community foundations may also impose restrictions on prospective grantees that counter your giving preferences. For example, they may disallow requests for general operating support or capital projects. They may avoid certain philosophies or ideas. Make sure you understand such grantmaking guidelines before donating.

If you create a designated fund, you can specify the beneficiary organization(s), and the timetable on which payments are made. But these are not DAFs, and if your designated organization goes out of business or changes its purpose, the community foundation can use your designated fund to support other organizations.

In many instances, donors and community foundations forge long-lasting and mutually rewarding relationships around a specific place to which they are both committed. Community foundations are no longer the only option, though, for donors who want to support their local community but don't have the assets, time, or interest to establish their own charitable entity. From a donor-intent perspective, it's wise to explore non-DAF giving options at community foundations with a good deal of caution.

Supporting organizations

Supporting organizations are, at first glance, attractive tools for donors who value simplicity, and seek an ongoing, perhaps multi-generational, relationship with the charity to be supported. Broadly defined, a Supporting Organization (SO) is a distinct legal entity that has a supporting relationship to a public charity. For example, the FSU Foundation Supporting Organization, which supports Fitchburg State University. Unlike private foundations, supporting organizations do not have to meet the public support test, and qualify as public charities even if they have only one donor. And unlike private foundations they are not subject to a minimum annual distribution requirement.

In terms of benefits to donors, supporting organizations:

- Save you from the paperwork, administrative, and reporting responsibilities and costs associated with a private foundation.
- Generate the public-charity tax advantages for contributions that are far more favorable than those of a private foundation.
- Free you from the management of day-to-day operations, since these are typically handled by the supported charity.
- Allow you to involve generations of family members, who may act as advisers to the supporting organization.

On the downside, a donor cannot control a supporting organization. The supported charity is guaranteed majority control or—at the very least—strong influence over the use of funds. Typically, a supporting organization will be respectful of your intentions while you are alive and seem likely to make additional gifts. But once you are no longer providing funding, supported organizations lose incentives to honor your intent. To reduce this risk, you can request the appointment of board members you know and trust. You may also include an exit clause in your agreement specifying that funds will go to an alternative organization if the supporting organization is unable to carry out your instructions. Neither of these measures is foolproof, though, and your giving priorities may well be disregarded over time. The Robertson Foundation's long dispute with Princeton University in the early 2000s—discussed in detail in Chapter 7—makes clear the potential danger to donor intent of using supporting organizations in your philanthropy.

Philanthropic partnerships

An intermediary organization can help philanthropists support an issue in partnership with other funders, using a portfolio approach instead of giving to a single organization. Examples include the Charter School Growth Fund, ClimateWorks, Give2Asia, the Global Fund for Women, Robin Hood Foundation, and Social Venture Partners. While collaborative funding, by definition, limits your donor intent, most funds offer donors some degree of control over the grantmaking process, varying according to the size of your contribution. Each fund sets its own minimum contributions and rules for exercising preferences, based on its mission and investment style.

Blue Meridian Partners, for example, seeks "to make a transformational impact on the lives of young people and families in poverty" by channelling pooled money to "promising interventions." Launched by the Edna McConnell Clark Foundation, Blue Meridian searches out organizations, evaluates their effects and ability to be expanded, develops a growth plan, provides management support, makes investments, monitors progress, and reports back to funding partners. The fund has raised $1.7 billion to date for its work. Each General Partner who contributes at least $50 million every five years has a vote in investment decisions. So-called Impact Partners contribute at least $15 million, with part of their money going into the partnership's central investment pool, and part able to be steered by the donor to groups in the Blue Meridian portfolio that are most appealing.

In all circumstances, your choice of a giving vehicle is always best done with input from your trusted advisers—wealth managers, accountants, and attorneys—and with close attention to your own values and philanthropic mission. Your advisers may have preconceived notions about what trust documents or articles of incorporation should include. Make sure they are listening to your wishes and concerns, and using the language that will best protect your goals.

Donors are increasingly utilizing multiple vehicles in pursuit of their objectives, so don't assume this is an either/or decision. If you are committed to protecting donor intent, then some of the vehicles discussed here have clear advantages over others—but only if you also take precautions to define your mission, consider alternatives to perpetuity, and select your board and staff members carefully.

Governance

No matter your mission, timeframe, giving vehicle, or other factors, choosing your first board is the most important decision you will make as a philanthropist concerned about donor intent. The people you select to shepherd your giving—particularly after your death—will make or break your donor intent. Your original board members will most likely work directly with you, learning not only what you want to accomplish, but also why and how. They will evaluate and name future trustees. Choose the right people, and you'll be well-positioned to see your mission properly executed. Choose the wrong people, and nothing will safeguard your intentions.

"If you've got the wrong people, no structure, no mission statement can hold them to donor intent," says Kim Dennis of the Searle Freedom Trust. "You can put things in writing very clearly," echoes Donn Weinberg, "but if you pick the wrong people, and they are motivated by their own ideologies and proclivities, then they'll start to change the meaning of words. If the early trustees are not honoring donor intent, the later ones will never do it."

Selecting the initial members for your board is tricky business and requires far more due diligence than picking your lawyer, golf buddy, or son-in-law. Donors often choose board members based on shared business activities or bloodlines, but both of those approaches, in isolation, can lead to disaster. Shared experience and family ties have their place in your decision. But neither should be your primary consideration. An "expert" with no interest in preserving donor intent might well convince other board members to take a direction in, say, education reform that is completely counter to your wishes. And family members often do the same. "You need to bring trustees on because their *philosophical* DNA matches yours, not necessarily their blood DNA," cautions Steve Moore of the Murdock Trust.

Because it will set the culture of your philanthropy for years to come, your first board must comprise people who truly understand that they are stewards of your mission. As Robert Bork noted in 1992, fidelity to donor intent in foundations demands "self-discipline in the service of the founder's, rather than one's own, moral purpose."

Cultivating board members

Choosing good board members takes time, and there is no shortcut. It's a matter of discernment and cultivation—more art than science. Finding strong candidates for your board requires getting to know them. It means discussing their thinking, over a long period of time, especially their thinking about the nature of philanthropy. It means posing questions that will uncover areas of agreement—and, equally important, disagreement. Do not settle for "yes" or "no" answers. Asking tough questions now may preserve the essence of your giftmaking in later years. The good news is that once you have them in place, the right board members can actually help you improve, refine, and define your giving.

It's advisable to put integrity, humility, and honesty high on your list of qualifications for board members. Indeed, place more emphasis on those traits than on professional qualifications. Candidates must be humble enough to subordinate their own interests and enthusiasms to the mission you set for them. They must be disciplined enough to constantly revisit and re-engage your vision. And they must be brave enough to take managerial, fiduciary, or legal steps to protect your intent when they feel it has been compromised. Remember, most people can be taught the mechanics of board service relatively quickly. The willingness to subordinate one's own desires in the service of another is a matter of character, usually developed over a lifetime.

Lawson Bader advises givers to find people they trust in their own generation—and, crucially, in a younger generation. "If you can actually bring people in at multiple generational levels, all of whom know you personally," he says, that will set up your board for long-term respect for donor intent.

> The people you select to shepherd your giving—particularly after your death— will make or break your donor intent.

And work directly and intensively with your first generation of trustees. They will benefit from working with you during your lifetime, learning your giving preferences, and precisely how you put your mission into action. And the give-and-take of grantmaking will help you ascertain that they are a strong fit as successor trustees. As Carl Helstrom, vice president for programs at the Lynde and Harry Bradley Foundation, puts it, "The best donor-intent stories are those where the donor was deeply involved in crafting not just the idea with trustees, but the actual grantmaking portfolio."

Dr. Phillips Charities and Dr. Phillips Inc. have granted close to $200 million to various community causes in Florida's Orange and Osceola counties, and nationally in support of free-enterprise advocates and property rights across the U.S. The original wealth creator, Dr. Philip Phillips, made his fortune in the first half of the twentieth century as one of the largest citrus growers in central Florida, then established a foundation to "help others help themselves." The first president, Jim Hinson, was a trusted business associate who worked directly with Phillips and his son Howard from 1957 onward. "When he enrolled new board members, Hinson really drilled down to some of their philosophies to determine if they had some ulterior motives, and to make sure they understood what the Dr. Phillips family donor intent was. Only after he had that buy-in was he comfortable bringing somebody on the board," says current president Kenneth Robinson.

As we've discussed, honoring donor intent doesn't mean that a board can't respond to new situations or opportunities. Adjustments are often necessary, and one enormous benefit of populating the first board with people whom the donor trusted, and who struggled alongside the donor to shape the foundation's grantmaking strategy, is that these shifts are made more intelligently and faithfully. Trustees intimately familiar with how the donor approached problems and analyzed potential solutions will be better able to navigate unexpected challenges and opportunities.

The founder of the Denver-based Daniels Fund did not include veterans' causes in his mission, but he was a veteran himself and admired the contributions of our armed services in preserving the nation's freedoms. "Over the years," explains Daniels Fund president Linda Childears, "we've had many opportunities to fund veterans' causes, and we as board members have looked at each other and said, 'We know Bill would love this.'" So the trustees eventually chose to help veterans within the context the donor had given them. They funded veteran-focused relief in areas that Daniels had favored: helping homeless, disadvantaged, and substance-abusing populations.

Board members need to become experts on their original donor. "You have to be a student of the donor," the president of Atlantic Philanthropies, Christopher Oechsli, told *Philanthropy* magazine in 2014. "The donor's intent consists of a range of elements: What motivated him, why did he want to give, what are the approaches, what are the values."

Considering a tiered structure for your board

Donor-intent concerns should be at the forefront of your decisionmaking in naming a board. But donor intent is not the only factor in the equation. Your board will also need competence in specific duties like understanding charitable problems and solutions, managing investments, complying with laws and codes, and overseeing professional staff. Having on your board some experts in certain fields such as medicine, public policy, or education reform could be helpful. But will such expert board members honor your intent?

Some donors have approached this issue by structuring their foundations with multi-tiered boards, with separate responsibilities assigned to each tier. The Searle Freedom Trust in Washington, D.C., has three distinct tiers that make up its board of directors. The first tier of trustees is responsible for stewarding the foundation's funds, including investment decisions. According to Dennis, this division of labor has proved invaluable because it allows the other two tiers of the board to focus on what they do best—giving money away in line with Searle's donor intent—without becoming distracted by the investment side of the equation.

Searle's second board tier consists of four grant advisers, chosen by Dan Searle himself, who are experts in the public-policy world and well versed in the subject areas of the foundation's grantmaking. These advisers are primarily public intellectuals with academic, policy, and think-tank management experience. They share Searle's general philosophical outlook—a commitment to individual freedom, economic liberty, personal responsibility, and traditional American values—and each worked closely with Searle during his lifetime. "They really know the ins and outs of the organizations we're funding," notes Dennis. These grant advisers, with the assistance of the professional staff, make the actual decisions about where and how the foundation will direct its funding.

> Board members must be humble and honest enough to subordinate their own enthusiasms to the mission you set for them.

The third tier of advisers consists of direct descendants of Daniel Searle. They are required to meet at least once annually with the grant advisers to review grants, and they have the power, on a unanimous basis, to overturn the decisions of the grant advisers. "Their role really comes into play when they insinuate something about Dan's intent," explains Dennis. "Sometimes, we'll be going back and forth over a grant decision and debating whether it's a good idea, whether it will be effective, and one of the family advisers will say flatly, 'Dan just wouldn't have supported this.' The family members are really helpful in that way."

None of these tiers has absolute control over the affairs of the foundation. This is the strength of the tiered approach—it separates board powers and responsibilities and delegates them to those best suited to perform them. To work well, however, this option still demands that you have the right people in place, and that they are, as Dennis notes, "committed to staying in their lanes."

Other founders have established tiered structures to safeguard donor intent. The John Templeton Foundation, for instance, is governed by both members and a board. The members—who include family representatives, Templeton Prize winners, and others—elect the board, where one-fourth of the trustees must be drawn from the Templeton family. Similarly, at the Earhart Foundation (which sunsetted in 2015) governance was divided between an all-family group of members and a non-family board of trustees. The former elected the latter, and that was their only role. You might also consider creating a tier of trusted "members" who alone are authorized to amend by-laws or approve board compensation. In considering any such changes to standard corporate structure, you should first consult your philanthropic attorneys.

Creating a tiered structure is no guarantee that your donor intent will be honored, or that "members" and "trustees" will automatically conform. It may even create resentment and power struggles. The tiered board structure is a complement to your other donor-intent safeguards, not a replacement for them. Whether you should follow this course of action is contingent, in part, on your foundation's size, mission, areas of giving, timeframe, and level of family involvement.

Compensating your board members

Compensating your board has positives and negatives. On the plus side, it can establish a working relationship with your trustees, with clear expectations that they will fulfill their responsibilities. The Peters Foundation, for example, chooses to pay its non-family trustees. While some of those board members refuse the compensation, Dan Peters believes that as a result of the offer, "they take their job seriously—we expect answers, and they give them." On the other side of the coin, boards who oversee foundations in perpetuity might become accustomed to the paycheck and "go along" with poor decisions just to ensure that it continues. That's why the Jaquelin Hume Foundation has purposefully decided not to pay its trustees for service. "Once you get somebody on the payroll, they want that money to continue. We pay their travel fees, but they don't get a salary," says the foundation's president, Jerry Hume.

You should understand that compensated board service (beyond reimbursement for expenses incurred) is a departure from the nonprofit tradition of volunteerism. Board members at grant-receiving public charities are generally expected to serve without compensation and to provide some level of financial support to the nonprofit organization. As William Schambra noted in *Philanthropy* in 2008, "Voluntary service… is regarded as an essential expression of human devotion to purposes beyond self-interest and a moral obligation of American citizenship." In fact, many foundations have adopted the policy of declining grant requests from public charities that compensate board members.

Critics of compensation argue that payments to trustees, which may legally be counted toward a foundation's mandatory annual payout, reduce the monies available for charitable grants. Foundation leaders also dispute the notion that compensation is necessary to recruit high-caliber board members or to make those board members more effective. Others suggest providing trustees with a limited amount of discretionary grantmaking as an alternative to direct payments. There is simply no one "right" answer to the question of board compensation and donors should identify the practice that best suits their needs.

With regard to donor intent, there are several powerful arguments for compensating your board:

- Whether they accept payment of $1 or $100,000, compensation clearly communicates to board members that they are working for the foundation and should uphold its mission, not pursue their own altruistic interests.
- Compensation widens the pool of available board members. If you want specialized expertise on your board, you may have to offer some form of payment in order to secure the service of people who will otherwise be unable to take part. Perhaps you want to include schoolteachers, or employees of religious charities, or creative workers with modest incomes on your board. They may be unable to spare the time as volunteers. Alternatively, compensation might be necessary to nab specialists like biomedical experts who are in short supply.

If you choose to compensate board members, keep several factors in mind. Paying your board members removes volunteer immunity. The federal Volunteer Protection Act of 1997 (as well as similar statutes in many states) provides broad—though not total—immunity from tort claims that might be filed against unpaid volunteers of nonprofit organizations. That can be viewed as a problem. At the same time, Harvey Dale, professor of philanthropy and law at New York University, has suggested that dropping this protection by paying compensation is "likely to increase the attention directors pay to fulfilling their fiduciary duties." (In any case, your foundation should purchase directors' and officers' liability insurance, often called "D&O," to provide indemnification for losses or defense costs suffered as a result of a legal action.)

Remember that to avoid running afoul of IRS requirements, pay must be "reasonable and necessary." Additionally, if you have family members on your board and you choose to pay them, extra judiciousness is warranted to avoid "self-dealing." One damning investigation by *The Boston Globe* revealed an indefensible compensation package offered by the Paul and Virginia Cabot Charitable Trust to Paul Cabot Jr. Between 1998 and 2002, Cabot was paid over $5.1 million for his service as a trustee, even though the foundation gave only about $2 million to charity during this period.

To guard against real abuses like that one, or more ambiguous issues, it's wise to put in writing some sort of job description for your board members. Explain the foundation's expectations for the work they are doing, the number of meetings they should attend, the number of hours they will spend on foundation business each week, etc. You may want to look at foundation board compensation surveys to compare your foundation with those that have a similar asset size. Your board meeting minutes should always record compensation decisions for directors and officers, including the data used to make those decisions. Finally, remember that compensation information is part of your foundation's tax filing and is readily available to the public.

Board compensation is one means of tapping individual self-interest for the purpose of preserving your intent. Whether it makes sense in your individual case primarily hinges on the demands of board service—the time and effort it takes for meetings, site visits, proposal reviews, and service on committees, among other responsibilities. You might conclude that compensation is simply unnecessary to attract well-qualified board members. Or you might decide that you specifically want people passionate enough about your mission to donate their time. You will have to strike the balance between pure volunteerism-based board service and enlightened self-interest in deciding what's appropriate for your unique circumstances.

Setting time limits on board service

"As a general rule, it's always easier to grow a board than to shrink it," says Keith Whitaker. "Once people are on there, it's very hard to dislodge them." A workaround that avoids the potential for confrontation and damaged relationships is a term-limit policy. After a set period—say, three years—board members must transition off the board unless they are re-elected to another term. Some policies add a hard limit to the number of years a board member might serve, but you may want to leave

Questions to ask prospective board members

You may already have several individuals in mind to serve as board members when you establish your philanthropy. Perhaps you have discussed your plans with them, outlining your interests and what you want to accomplish. They may be family members, long-time friends, or business associates with whom you've worked closely and have a relationship built on mutual trust. What you are considering now, though, is a very different undertaking, and one that may last several decades or even longer. At the heart of good governance, reminds Virginia Esposito of the National Center for Family Philanthropy, is "building the board your foundation deserves." Don't take shortcuts in assessing possible candidates.

Here are some questions that can help you assess candidates:

- What do you know about this foundation (trust, donor-advised fund, etc.)? How does our mission resonate with you?
- Have you had prior board experiences? Have you had any experience related to our mission?
- How do you see your responsibilities as a foundation board member? What role does the board play in protecting donor intent?
- How do you see the role of a living donor at the foundation?
- What personal/professional/intellectual qualities do you think will make a great board member for this foundation?
- What role do you think you would play on the board?
- How do you typically go about making decisions in a group setting?
- How do you think a trustee should go about questioning conventional wisdom or what appears to be the majority opinion?
- What has given you the most pleasure in your personal giving? How do you choose among competing interests?
- How do you see philanthropy solving the problems this foundation is trying to address? What impact do you think we can have? What challenges do you think we are facing?
- Will you be able to contribute the necessary amount of time to this endeavor?

• Do you have any concerns about joining the board?

There are certain types of board members that donors should probably avoid. The ideal board member should be neither too aggressive nor too passive. An overly aggressive board member can lead to counter-productive friction, or substitution of his or her views for the donor's preferences. A too-passive board member may not be willing to stand on principle on important questions including donor intent. Individuals who see foundation board service as an opportunity to bolster personal prestige are not likely to place the foundation's—or donor's—interest above their own. And a too-forceful personality may end up dominating the board, discouraging others from sharing their opinions, and cutting you off from valuable advice.

open the option for well-aligned board members, rich in relational and institutional knowledge about you and your giving, to serve for long periods. Even without overall caps, simple term limits offer an opportunity to make changes when necessary. Some boards choose to apply this policy only to the term of the chairman and not the individual members, and so long as there are no concerns about adherence to donor intent, this can be a healthy way of sharing the burden of leadership.

Stopping short of establishing firm term limits, there are many "creative ways to bring people into the fold without handing them the reins," Whitaker notes. If you are seeking knowledgeable advice around particular issues or communities, or connections with other funders, structures are available that don't include governing authority. You may, for example, establish an advisory council for one of your grantmaking areas. In a family foundation you may create a junior or adjunct board for family members who wish to participate in your philanthropy but will not have a vote in decisions of the governing board. Non-voting advisers may be permitted to make grants up to a certain amount annually so long as they fall within the foundation's mission and do not violate donor intent.

Planning for board succession

It's one thing to pick board members whom you trust while you're living. It's another to plan successfully for board succession after you've passed away. Donor-intent violations often occur during these moments, when founding trustees hand their authority to the next generation. Particularly if you intend your foundation to operate in perpetuity, it is crucial to define the process of choosing successor trustees.

Board succession should unfold according to a predetermined plan, one that you have carefully considered with your original board members. The sudden loss of a key individual should not cause a crisis. The same qualities of character and commitment to donor intent that you sought in your first-generation board members, and your careful process of cultivating them, ought to be emulated in choosing future generations of the board. Discussing this process with your founding board members and committing to paper the specific qualifications for future leadership is vitally important in transmitting your intentions. Even smart founders often overlook this. "Bill Daniels said, 'Here's a list of buddies that you ought to call on when you need to replace directors.' I think it would have been very helpful if he had said, 'When you look for future directors, look for these qualities,' instead of saying, 'Look for these people,'" says Linda Childears.

If you establish a foundation in perpetuity or set a sunset date several decades after your death, keep in mind the importance of age diversity on your original board. If the men and women whom you appoint in your lifetime as board members are all of a similar age, they may leave the board at about the same time. Imagine what would happen if there were a sudden and complete turnover of long-time board members and the next board included no one who had worked directly with you. To prevent jeopardizing your intent, stagger the ages of your first board members and discuss with them the importance of continuing that practice.

The story of the M. J. Murdock Charitable Trust underscores the importance of getting your first board right from the start. Jack Murdock never married and had no children, yet his donor intent never veered off course. It certainly could have happened: Murdock's will established a broad mission statement for his giving—to nurture and enrich the educational, social, and spiritual life of individuals, families, and communities. That statement was wide enough to pose interpretation challenges for future trustees. After the Murdock Charitable Trust was officially established in 1975, the first executive action of the trustees was to comb through Murdock's checkbook to see where he gave money himself. Clearer directions drawn from that practical record, and from conversations with those who knew Murdock well, empowered trustees to fully understand what type of philanthropy was appropriately "Murdockish." Focused on grantmaking in the Pacific Northwest and

Alaska, the Murdock Charitable Trust has to date allocated nearly a billion dollars to arts and culture, education, health and human services, and science research.

Establishing board policies to protect your intent

So far, this chapter has addressed how to recruit, train, and retain strong members for your board of directors. The next step is to establish powerful operational board policies to preserve your intent and foster loyalty to your philanthropic wishes. Below are several steps you may take:

Review your mission statement at board meetings

Many foundations choose a regular time—such as once a year at annual board meetings—to read their mission statement. Instituting this sort of ritual reminds trustees of their founder's original purpose and, through discussion, gives them a chance to evaluate how they're measuring up in current grant decisions.

"Our founder, James Duke, required his trustees to read the entire indenture, out loud, once a year," says Eugene Cochrane, former president of the Duke Endowment. "They do this every February at their board meeting. It takes about 45 minutes, and it's a wonderful way for the board and senior management to hear his voice and to focus on his wishes."

At the Daniels Fund, most of the directors have been video-recorded discussing their relationship with the founder, Bill Daniels, and how they understand his donor intent. Additionally, the fund's bylaws require that time is set aside at each annual meeting to reflect on Daniels and his philosophy of giving, and each year a director is asked to prepare a presentation discussing Daniels' intentions. Some foundations begin each board meeting by sharing a story, correspondence, or testimonial about a grant that is manifestly advancing the foundation's mission.

Other foundations have legacy statements printed at the top of their meeting agenda or in the front of their board book. Or they schedule a portion of meetings to review and discuss founding documents and reflect on what was most important to the donor. Still others invite past board chairs or senior family members to discuss grantmaking history and their recollections of the founding wealth creator. For family foundations, a powerful tool to bind future generations to donor intent is an oral history—or better, a video—of the founder speaking about his or her motivation for engaging in philanthropy. Whatever model you choose, your goal is to create a pervasive culture that honors donor intent. When staff and grantees see that your board takes seriously your philanthropic wishes, they better understand that the same is expected of them.

Require board members to sign a statement
Some philanthropies require board members to sign a statement of donor intent. It might be part of a broader ethics and governance training session, or it might stand on its own. For example, the Daniels Fund requires its board members to sign a Statement of Commitment and Understanding. After reviewing a detailed set of documents describing the life, values, character, and intentions of the founder, directors are asked to ratify the following:

> Signing this document affirms your commitment to preserve Bill Daniels' donor intent and his personal style of conducting business (as described in this document). You agree to set aside your personal views or preferences when acting on behalf of the Daniels Fund. It is the Board's responsibility to ensure that the Daniels Fund most effectively fulfills Bill Daniels' intentions and remains true to his ideals. You also acknowledge that you have read this document and understand its importance in guiding the efforts of the Daniels Fund.

This document, Childears notes, makes clear to new board members that foundation leadership views their appointments with keen seriousness. "We vet new board members like we're giving them the keys to our house—because we are giving them the keys to Bill's house," she says.

Create trustee apprenticeships
You might ease in new board members by apprenticing them. The Samuel Roberts Noble Foundation in Ardmore, Oklahoma, developed a practice of naming apprentices, called "advisery directors," who attend and participate in all board meetings. Advisery directors have no vote in actions of the board but otherwise exercise all privileges, powers, rights, and duties of directors. They keep abreast of all board activities and participate in board discussions. Advisery directors serve annual terms with no limit to the number of consecutive terms they may serve. Age limits applicable to directors also apply to advisery directors. Some "apprentices" may progress to board membership. If you plan to operate your foundation in perpetuity, implementing board apprenticeships might play an important role in your succession planning.

Require peer review among board members
Creating a review process to assess whether board members are actively respecting and honoring donor intent, when combined with appropriate follow-up by the board chair, can be a valuable tool for both evaluation and ongoing education. An assessment might also reveal whether each board member:

- Is knowledgeable concerning the foundation's mission and has the necessary skills to see that it is carried out.
- Devotes enough time, thought, and resources to achieve the mission.
- Has the necessary relationships with people and organizations to advance the foundation's mission.

As noted above, your bylaws should include provisions for term limits of board members, or a requirement that each member be re-elected at a given point. Re-election can encourage board members to reflect on their fidelity to donor intent and be more conscientious about carrying it out.

> Your goal should be to create a pervasive culture that honors donor intent —board, staff, grantees all taking your philanthropic wishes seriously.

Establish board removal powers
Some foundations choose to give supermajorities of their boards the power to remove an individual member. Others vest that power in a single individual, such as a family member, family adviser, or outside entity (such as a public charity with whom you work closely). As explained in more detail below, the Roe Foundation has given the Mont Pelerin Society and the Philadelphia Society—two organizations which founding benefactor Thomas Roe trusted because they shared his philosophical outlook—standing to sue the foundation's board members if they depart from his intent. Be advised, however, that such "watchdog" entities may also take a direction that veers from your intent.

Ensure that individual grants bolster your intent

Your goal should be to create a culture in your foundation that instinctively honors donor intent—from your board chair through your administrative staff. One of the best ways to do this is by ensuring that your grant awards honor your intent while you are around.

- *Develop grantmaking guidelines with donor intent in mind*
  Use your grantmaking guidelines as another way to communicate your intent to program officers, other staff members, and prospective grantees. Clearly articulated grantmaking guidelines remove pressure from your board members—who will likely be the frequent recipients of off-mission requests from outside parties—and enable them to decline such requests.

- *Evaluate proposed grants to ensure they align with donor intent*
  At the Arthur N. Rupe Foundation, all grant evaluations written by the program officer include a section on how the grant advances the foundation's mission. The board reviews these evaluations to ensure that the foundation's grantmaking is in line with the founder's intentions. The Templeton Foundation also requires that proposed grants demonstrably relate to the original purposes of the foundation as stated in its charter.

- *Give board members discretionary grants*
  Some foundations, in an effort to recognize their trustees and directors for their commitment and remove the temptation of proposing pet projects or other grants that do not align with the foundation's mission to the board, give their directors discretionary grantmaking authority over a pre-determined amount. The John M. Olin Foundation, for example, gave its directors what are sometimes called "board" or "chairman" grants, as do many other foundations. The Olin Foundation allowed each board member to make grants of up to $25,000 (eventually the figure became $100,000). Some foundations restrict board discretionary grants to the mission of the foundation. Others leave them open-ended. Family foundations tied to a specific place may offer such grantmaking opportunities to family trustees who no longer reside there. It may be pragmatic to create an outlet for modest discretionary grants, provided they do not distract the board from the stated philanthropic mission. As a policy intended to help secure

donor intent, however, thoughtful oversight is necessary to prevent off-mission grants from morphing into grants which directly counter donor intent.

Scatter reminders of donor intent around your building
If you have a building or office devoted to your foundation, you should consider using this physical space to enshrine your donor intent. The Daniels Fund is one of the best examples of this—its headquarters in Denver is filled with memorabilia describing the life, mission, and values of Bill Daniels.

At the Connelly Foundation, artwork, pictures, and objects dot the office as visual cues to donor intent. "You can't really look anywhere here without seeing visible reminders of the charity and values of John and Josephine Connelly," says Tom Riley. "It's a benefit for the staff, trustees, grantees, and anybody else who is here to make the Connellys' presence more palpable and less abstract."

> If you plan to operate your foundation
> in perpetuity, the ultimate question is
> who or what will hold staff accountable
> if they depart from your charitable mission.

Cheryl Taylor, president and CEO of the Foellinger Foundation in Fort Wayne, Indiana, agrees with this approach. "We have a lot of visual cues to donor intent for people coming in from the outside—and equally important, if not more so, for our board," adding that an enormous photo of Helene and Esther Foellinger in the board room sets the tone for every meeting held there.

Establishing external safeguards for your intent
Even with sound internal policies and procedures, your foundation will have very few external defenses for your donor intent heading into the future. You may have an ally in your state's attorney general, who has the statutory authority to oversee all charitable organizations. But your attorney general may or may not intervene if a donor-intent dispute develops. And if he or she does intervene,

GOVERNANCE

the process of weighing donor intent against the perceived public interest has resulted in a mixed legal and judicial record.

If you plan to operate your foundation in perpetuity, the ultimate question is who or what will hold your board members accountable if they depart from your charitable mission. Some donors have instituted external safeguards for their intent. We describe three of these below. (One caveat to keep in mind: few such safeguards have been put to a legal test. Still, there may be good reasons to create such mechanisms.)

Give standing to outside parties
Thomas Roe was a South Carolina businessman who used his philanthropy to help establish a movement of state-focused, free-market think tanks across the country. He began with the launch of the South Carolina Policy Council in 1986. Roe was a judicious guardian of donor intent when he established his foundation: clearly spelling out his beliefs and wishes in the founding documents, and requiring grantees to pledge to uphold the mission of the foundation in their work.

Still concerned that the worst might happen, Roe named two organizations—the Mont Pelerin Society and the Philadelphia Society—as "watchdogs" of his foundation. He granted them and their directors standing to challenge his foundation in court, in case it ran contrary to his stated donor intent at any point in the future. Roe also insisted that these two organizations, in addition to being granted standing to sue, remain substantial beneficiaries of the foundation, receiving annual grants. This second provision—giving two organizations meaningful contributions each year—makes them, in effect, quasi-beneficiaries with a special interest in the conduct of the foundation.

Roe was active in both organizations during his lifetime, and so had good reason to believe they shared his philosophical outlook. Moreover, he had faith that their members and donors would hold them accountable to their missions, so that if the Roe Foundation ever changed course, the board members of the Mont Pelerin Society and the Philadelphia Society would step in to resolve the issue.

Whether or not a judge would give either organization standing in court is an open question. Nevertheless, the publicity surrounding such an attempted lawsuit might serve as adequate deterrent to potentially wayward Roe Foundation trustees, and the inclusion of these third parties in the foundation's bylaws is a not-so-subtle reminder to its trustees that they can be held to account by outside parties.

Incorporate sympathetic organizations into your board

A second option is to specify in your bylaws or founding documents that certain organizations that share your values should be represented on your board. Under this scenario, board representatives from third-party organizations can ensure that the philanthropy is abiding by the donor's intentions as stated in the mission statement. As board members they will have governance power, and standing to bring suit, if the organization takes a direction contrary to its stated purpose. Some observers have even suggested that donors stipulate that a majority of board members be drawn from one or more charitable organizations that share the foundation's mission, to act as watchdogs of the donor's priorities.

There are, however, serious potential drawbacks to consider in giving third-party organizations influence over your grantmaking entity:

- Such organizations may themselves drift from their missions in ways you cannot anticipate. It is important to consider carefully the organizations you involve in your board, including their history and their own provisions for ensuring that they pursue their stated purpose.
- Representatives from outside organizations may cultivate financial support for their own organizations or accede to board decisions counter to donor intent to maintain such support.
- The organization may simply cease to exist. In this instance, a provision should require the foundation's board to choose another representative organization, ideally from a list you provided. In that way you can maintain the positive influence you sought when you designated that board seat.

Institute donor-intent audits

The John Templeton Foundation is a prime example of a philanthropy that has instituted special procedures to reinforce donor intent. Every five years, the foundation undergoes an external audit to measure how well it is adhering to its founder's wishes. The board of trustees selects three organizations who work in focus areas identified by John Templeton. Each organization then chooses an individual from its ranks to be an auditor.

The Templeton Foundation ensures that each auditor understands the core principles and focus areas of the foundation, and what the donor intended. The auditors then review grants approved during the previous five years and determine whether they honor donor intent. Finally, the auditors issue a report to the board of trustees, and the board reports to the members of the foundation.

While the process is more detailed than can be fully explained here, its impact is clear. President Heather Dill explains that "The real benefit of the compliance audit is not so much the process itself and all the particularities of the audit, but that we as management are always thinking about what the founder would want. Would he categorize this project as we're categorizing it, and would our reason be convincing to an auditor? So it forces us always to think about donor intent, it forces us to read the governing documents on a regular basis, and it forces us to read a lot of books that my grandfather wrote in which he further articulated his vision." She warns that "The audit process is not for every organization or every donor because it does mean we need certain staff members and systems to monitor all the details, but this is how my grandfather wanted it."

Achieving balance with your safeguards

All recommendations for board policies come with a caveat: your internal and external donor-intent protections shouldn't be so severe as to stifle engagement by your board members. Trustees must have a sense of what their title suggests—that you have some faith in their judgment. Board members who do not believe their contributions are valued may not invest time on your board, or offer much effort or imagination, or feel true allegiance to your mission. Your goal should be to create policies that inspire and guide board members, more than question their integrity or abilities. As Paul Rhoads, president of the Grover Hermann Foundation, advises, "One wants to encourage future trustees, and establish an esprit de corps that develops loyalty to the foundation's mission."

That very loyalty suggests that you give serious consideration to one critical area of flexibility—that of foundation lifespan. If you have set up your foundation in perpetuity, you may want to give your trustees the authority to sunset it at some point in the future. As discussed in Chapter 5, the trustees of both the Avi Chai and Earhart foundations did just that rather than extend their founda-tions' existence beyond the lives of board members who had known their donors personally. Board members who truly understand the importance of honoring donor intent will be loathe to risk violation in the future and will welcome the opportunity to fulfill their obli-gation as the stewards of your legacy.

The special governance challenge of living donors

Personal relationships can obscure responsibilities and roles for board members—a trustee may know the living donor well from business or otherwise, but not be aware of the donor's priorities and expectations. Living donors must take this into account when selecting board members and establishing policies and procedures for their philanthropy. It is your responsibility to articulate, on a regular basis, your preferred operating style, your goals for your philanthropy, and what strategies you prefer. The more you work closely with your board members, the better they will understand your thinking around the issues that concern you.

Regarding governance, a living donor must address these questions before selecting and convening a board:

- What is the role you wish to play in the governance of your philanthropy? Will you join the board? Chair the board? If you don't chair the board, what sort of relationship will you maintain with the board chair?
- Will all board decisions be subject to your approval, including grant and investment decisions? Will this allow other board members to fulfill their legal and fiduciary duties? Can they participate effectively in a wide range of decisionmaking between the extremes of rubber-stamping or overriding a donor's intentions? What do you expect your board members to bring to the table in terms of advice and decisionmaking in order to enhance and advance your donor intent?
- If you choose to share governance with your board in a structure where all votes are equal, then what precautions must you take to ensure that your donor intent is honored and not frustrated, both during your lifetime and afterwards?

Hiring, Operations, and Grantmaking Consistent with Donor Intent

Your mission is only as strong as your people. And selecting your trustees is only the first step. Ensuring that staff are aligned with your mission is also crucial. Staff play a significant role in either honoring—or disregarding—your intent because they are on the front lines, meeting with potential grant recipients, interacting with the community, and developing grant recommendations. Every day, staff members make decisions, large and small, that will determine whether your organization fulfills its mission. Professional staff can exert more practical power than trustees or even donors if there is a passive approach to governance.

As Childears states, "There is an old saying: *personnel is policy.* What that means is it's necessary to hire staff members who are philosophically in line with your mission and will work to achieve it. Each new staff member you hire, at any level of the organization, is a vote you are casting in favor of donor intent—or in favor of its dismantling."

After the Daniels Fund successfully resolved a donor-intent crisis in the early 2000s involving wayward staff members and several like-minded trustees, the foundation adopted a more careful hiring and onboarding process for new employees. (See Chapter 8.) Under current policy, each proposed hire must be approved by the president, and she specifically evaluates fidelity to donor intent as one criterion in her decision. After hiring, a new staff member must undergo a several-hour donor-intent orientation. Then they go to work in a headquarters filled with memorabilia and mementos to Bill Daniels' philanthropic intent and legacy. "Our staff for the most part view Bill as a sort of idol, which is exactly what I want," Childears says. "That's the effect I'm after."

At the Bradley Foundation—where staffers are several generations removed from Lynde and Harry Bradley—donor intent remains an active concern. "We still call on Lynde and Harry," says Richard Graber, the foundation's president and CEO. "Were they still sitting at the table, what would they do in a particular situation?"

The Connelly Foundation hired a professional historian to create a monograph on the charitable giving of John and Josephine Connelly, and every new staff member gets a copy. "A big part of onboarding new staff members is a deliberate education in donor intent—not just the 'what' but the 'why,' the donors' values and how they've been applied over the years," says Riley.

As a donor, you want to bring on staff who will enhance the effectiveness of your philanthropy. Yet you must also be alert to the ways in which staff can easily allow their own values and agendas to redirect the organization. Take these steps to increase the likelihood of successful hires:

Choose the right CEO
Aside from your choice of board, picking the man or woman who will lead your foundation is the most crucial decision you will make. Donn

Weinberg calls this step "the most important job" of your board. "If the CEO is the right pick, then the donor's wishes will be observed," he says.

Wise donors frequently search for CEOs outside the world of foundations, choosing from people experienced with the donor's work, favorite charities, and personality. "If I were in charge of hiring my replacement at the Daniels Fund," says Childears, "I would make sure he or she had been responsible for managing payroll somewhere. It would need to be someone who truly appreciates what it takes to amass this type of fortune. Most foundation colleagues would cringe at the thought of business experience, but I think it's really important."

No matter where your search leads you—even among friends and family—be diligent in making your decision. You may know an individual's professional credentials but not his core values, her personal attributes but not her philosophy of private philanthropy. No matter how eager you are to get your grantmaking off the ground, don't risk hiring a CEO who is not aligned with your beliefs and goals. Remember that this will be the individual responsible for articulating your vision to others and managing the grantmaking to implement your mission. Your relationship with your CEO—like your relationship with your board—must be anchored in trust.

Evaluate beliefs, philosophy, and integrity for all staff members
You and your foundation's executive should take time to understand the philosophical underpinnings of each potential staff member. Pay particular attention to program staff who will play a significant role in your grantmaking, but know your administrative staff as well. Don't assume that administrative staff have little influence on office culture and practice. "You've got to emphasize values and passion," says Al Mueller. "If real estate is about location, location, location, in philanthropy it's got to be values, values, values."

Create a culture of fidelity to donor intent
Although digressions from donor intent should be addressed immediately, your long-term goal isn't to create a culture of fear. Instead, you want shared values, genuine care, and reverence for central principles. Look to build traditions and practices within your operations that create loyalty to your intentions among the people of your organization. Cultivate your staff members over time. Invest in their professional development and give them increased responsibility as they show a greater appreciation and understanding of your foundation's mission.

Consider time-limiting your foundation

Sunsetting can be a simple solution to concerns about future staff composition in the absence of a living donor. One of the reasons the Jaquelin Hume Foundation has decided to sunset, for example, is to allay concerns about the direction in which successor staff might take the organization. If you choose this route, be sure to have attractive incentives in place to retain key staff up to the shutdown—in keeping with the examples of the Avi Chai and Earhart foundations sketched earlier.

Establishing grantmaking principles and practices

Grant compliance is an important concern for all donors, but particularly for those with well-defined values and mission statements. Chapter 7 will explore the special challenges of giving to colleges and universities, but there are several principles and practices that should guide you and your designated representatives in your oversight of grants.

> The goal isn't to create a culture of fear.
> Instead, you want shared values,
> genuine care, and reverence
> for central principles.

Know your recipients

Investigate each potential grant recipient. Familiarize yourself with its mission, leadership, financials, and programs. Make site visits. Depending on your level of commitment to the organization, get involved in the life of the organization by attending programs and functions. Trust your instincts. Do you feel comfortable placing your charitable dollars with this organization? Is it the one that will make the best use of your money? Or is there a similar organization accomplishing its mission more effectively? "Grant compliance happens best when you've done the work upfront to make sure you're partnering with an organization that really believes in what you're trying to do and isn't just trying to game your system in order to get money," says Keith Whitaker of Wise Counsel Research. "The best compliance is the investigatory work, the due diligence, the time commitment needed to get to know a grantee."

Make short-term commitments (or long-term ones in short segments)
All nonprofits experience change over time. People come and go. Mission statements shift and drift. Organizations might even shutter altogether. That's why making shorter-term commitments—rather than long-term endowments—in your grantmaking is one of the best steps you can take. If you'd like to make a long-term commitment to an organization, try periodic grants that will be based on recent performance to give you leverage in grant compliance.

Create a suitably detailed grant agreement
Depending on the nature of your gift, put a gift contract or grant agreement in place. There are many examples of gift contracts, some more complicated than others. Avoid micromanaging, but ensure that both parties have a clear understanding of expectations, restrictions, and reporting requirements. Grant agreements can also outline in advance a means of resolving disputes.

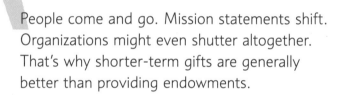

People come and go. Mission statements shift.
Organizations might even shutter altogether.
That's why shorter-term gifts are generally
better than providing endowments.

Consider an intermediary organization
You may consider making your gift through an intermediary organization that will serve to enforce your intentions over time. A third-party organization can ensure compliance standards in your absence, prior to disbursing funds. Likewise, you may consider naming organizations as contingent beneficiaries if the original grant recipient fails to live up to the terms of the gift agreement.

Realize the limitations of grant compliance
Even with a grant agreement in place, once you make the gift, the money is no longer yours. It's far easier to create a good working relationship with an organization before making a gift than to try, after the fact, to force it to comply. It takes time, even years, to understand what you can realistically achieve through your grantmaking within a given field or

with a particular organization or group of organizations. Many donors make large gifts early on that they later come to regret. Take time to learn about the field where you are working, the people and institutions doing the work, and try to formulate realistic expectations grounded in experience rather than slick marketing brochures, attractive websites, or utopian ideas about what your gift can accomplish.

Giving Wisely to Colleges and Universities

Higher education can be among the most rewarding and meaningful areas for your donor dollars. This sector attracts some of the heaviest philanthropic support of any sector, with private giving to colleges and universities now totaling around $50 billion annually. Generous alumni and others have allowed numerous universities to build up endowments containing billions of dollars.

Though popular, higher education is also the most challenging sector for donor intent and grant compliance. Unless you are careful, college and university administrations may ignore, creatively interpret, disregard, or directly violate your donor intent. "Universities can be difficult about complying with donor intent because they have such a wall built around themselves," cautions donor Tom Lewis of the T. W. Lewis Foundation. "They often don't want anyone to interfere with their agenda."

For alumni donors in particular, "higher-education philanthropy is more emotionally tricky than other types of giving," warns Jacqueline Pfeffer Merrill, director of the Campus Free Expression Project at the Bipartisan Policy Center. "People have an emotional pull to their alma mater, and it can be easy not to think strategically. Our advice to donors is to approach their giving without rose-colored glasses on."

Take the case of Robert Morin, a 1963 graduate of the University of New Hampshire who worked in the school's Diamond Library for five decades. Thanks to a lifetime of frugality, the humble librarian had amassed an estate worth $4 million at his death. He donated the entirety of it to his alma mater, with only $100,000 earmarked for his beloved library.

Free to decide how to spend $3.9 million, the University of New Hampshire drew withering criticism for dedicating $1 million of Morin's estate to a new video scoreboard for the school's football stadium. Another $2.5 million funded a career center. The remaining $400,000 is still unallocated. One alumnus described these administrative decisions as "a complete disgrace to the spirit and memory of Robert Morin." UNH administrators claimed that Morin had, in fact, become a football fan in the last fifteen months of his life, while critics complained that the school was "deceptively connecting a fragment of Morin's life to its football splurge." The truth was that Morin himself had left the university free to spend the bulk of his donation however it chose.

One of the most publicized donor-university skirmishes is the dispute between Princeton University and the Robertson family. In 1961, Marie Robertson—an heir to the A&P grocery fortune—and her husband Charles gave Princeton A&P stock worth $35 million to endow a supporting organization (the Robertson Foundation) whose purpose was to educate graduate students "for careers in government service." The endowment's value mushroomed to $930 million by 2007, by which time it was being used to fund most of the graduate programs in the Woodrow Wilson School of Public and International Affairs. The Robertsons' children concluded that Princeton was not fulfilling the terms of the endowment and filed suit. A PriceWaterhouseCoopers forensic audit of the Robertson Foundation accounts revealed that Princeton had, in fact, misused more than $100 million in earmarked funds.

After spending nearly $90 million combined on legal fees without even going to trial, the Robertson heirs and the university reached a settlement in 2009 in which Princeton agreed to return $100 million. After the family's legal fees were paid, a bit more than $50 million went to fund a new Robertson Foundation for Government that is independent of Princeton and allows Robertson family members to honor the donors' original intent at other academic institutions. Princeton took the remaining funds and rolled them into its over-all endowment—which now stands at $26 billion—and the original Robertson Foundation was dissolved. Both sides claimed victory, but the $100 million returned to the Robertson family by Princeton constitutes the largest award on behalf of donor intent in history. The lead plaintiff in the suit, William Robertson, issued a statement call-ing the settlement "a message to nonprofit organizations of all kinds throughout our country that donors expect them to abide by the terms of the designated gifts or suffer the consequences."

What might you do to prevent misuse like that of the Robertson gift?

• Avoid using a supporting organization as the repository for funds. As noted in Chapter 4, a donor cannot control a supporting organization, and the supported charity is guaranteed majority control or—at the very least—significant influence over your grantmaking. The Robertson Foundation board had four members appointed by Princeton and three family members.
• Eschew a perpetual endowment altogether. The Robertsons' commitment to Princeton could have been for a limited term, with funds made available on a schedule which allowed for periodic formal reviews. Even a term of 20 years gives a donor more opportunities to ask questions and evaluate outcomes, and serves to keep grantees on track if they seek renewal.
• Consider the impact of changing relationships. Neither Marie and Charles Robertson nor the college administrators and faculty who accepted their gift were parties to the 2002 lawsuits. The

familiarity and trust that had existed between Princeton and the donors in 1961 had long eroded, dealing one more heavy blow to the already wobbly structure of a perpetual endowment within a supporting organization.

Another example of donor intent gone awry is a grant made in the 1980s by the Carl F. Herzog Foundation to the University of Bridgeport in Connecticut to endow nursing scholarships for needy students. Facing a steady enrollment decline, the university closed its nursing program in 1991 and reallocated the gift to its general endowment. When the foundation sued, the Connecticut Supreme Court upheld the university's action because the foundation had failed to include in the gift agreement a reversionary clause indicating the gift should be returned if the nursing program was discontinued—another lesson for donors. Ironically, the school restored its nursing program in the 2000s.

Unless you are very careful, college administrators may ignore, creatively interpret, disregard, or directly violate your donor intent.

Legal disputes between donors and universities continue. In an early 2018 high-profile case, the Pearson Family Members Foundation filed a lawsuit against the University of Chicago claiming the institution failed to abide by a 2015 grant agreement. In that year the foundation committed a $100 million grant to create the Pearson Institute for the Study and Resolution of Global Conflicts in the Harris School of Public Policy. Now Pearson family members are seeking to reclaim the $22.9 million already paid on the grant, claiming the university failed to hire a full-time institute director and high-quality faculty, develop a curriculum, or schedule an annual forum according to the timeline spelled out in a 60-page gift agreement. The university has denied the accusations in a public statement noting, "In the short time since its formation, the institute has hosted dozens of events, enrolled more than 200 students in courses related to the study of global conflict, and fostered an engaged community of scholars."

The university is clear in proclaiming its prerogatives: "All academic and hiring decisions are the sole purview of the university and its faculty, guided by the principle of academic freedom." The Pearsons, however, have challenged both the timing and qualifications of those hired for their institute. They see this dispute as "a cautionary tale that should give pause to any…donor who is considering granting a university any amount of money."

In another recent clash, donor Roger Lindmark sued his alma mater, St. John's University in Collegeville, Minnesota, demanding the return of his $300,000 gift to the school to create a summer fellowship for rising seniors to complete a substantive research paper on corporate-business ethics. From the time the gift was finalized in 2010 until the fall of 2017, Lindmark claimed, he received only a handful of thank-you letters from scholarship recipients and no information on the research conducted. In the fall of 2017, when he demanded to see the 16 papers produced, he received only 10 of them and was shocked to see that most of them were not on the subject he specified. "The papers that were produced were on topics totally outside corporate-business ethics," Lindmark told MPR News. "One paper was done on soil conservation. Another was done on romance in the workplace. Another one was about providing solar power energy to low-income families. Another paper was produced on wonderment in the classroom." One of Lindmark's lawsuit exhibits was a scholarship recipient's five-page paper explaining why he couldn't complete the assignment! Nonetheless, Lindmark lost his case when courts ruled that the endowment he created was an irrevocable gift governed by the laws of Minnesota, and that only the state's attorney general had standing to sue.

Both parties contributed to this outcome. Lindmark knew what he meant by "corporate-business ethics," but failed to spell it out clearly in the gift agreement. He also let too many years pass before demanding copies of the fellowship recipients' work. For its part, the university provided little—if any—faculty oversight to the Lindmark Fellows to ensure that paper topics were in line with the donor's wishes. Today the Lindmark Fellowship website advises applicants that "the research topic of 'professional business ethics' is broadly construed."

Even when donors do a good job of clarifying their wishes with universities, their intent may be violated. In 2016, Westminster College in Fulton, Missouri, petitioned a court for access to $12.6 million in restricted endowment grants to fund its general operating budget, in violation of the donors' original wishes for those grants. During the hearing it came to light that Westminster's president had already withdrawn half of those restricted funds without a court order, and was in fact asking to access more money. The court grudgingly granted the college's petition, but mandated a full payback-with-interest schedule, a policy that required approval from the board of trustees to access endowment funds, and the submission of Westminster's annual independent audit to the state attorney general for several years.

At Ohio State University, alumnus Jeffrey Moritz, son of Michael Moritz for whom the College of Law is named, is disputing a fee levied by the university on a $30.3 million endowment created by his father in 2001. The terms of the gift were specific: all the funds were to support four chaired professorships and 30 annual law school scholarships. In 2016, however, Moritz learned that OSU was distributing only 12-16 awards each year and that the endowment held only $21.9 million. OSU first claimed that the drop was entirely due to the recession, but financial reports eventually revealed that about $3 million had been taken from the Moritz fund to support the university's development operations. The 1-1.3% annual fee—which the university had begun charging in 1994—appeared nowhere in the 2001 gift agreement and the Moritz family claims the school never told them about the fee which began to appear in gift agreements only in 2008. They are demanding that OSU return $3 million to the endowment, but it is unclear whether Jeffrey Moritz and his family will succeed. Both OSU and the state's attorney general are fighting his attempt to reopen his father's estate so the probate court can appoint him as administrator to enforce the original gift agreement.

Wise giving in higher education

Fortunately, there are examples of donors successfully navigating the tumultuous waters of higher-education giving. It requires planning and effort on your part, but the payback is worth the work. Jack Miller, chairman of the Jack Miller Center, has a clear message for donors to colleges: "If you aren't prepared to protect donor intent, what you intend doesn't mean much." Three strategies can help:

- Establish with the university a clear grant agreement that protects donor rights.
- Ally yourself with a university employee who is genuinely interested in what your support will fund, and maintain strong working relationships with faculty and administrators.

- Channel your gifts through campus allies rather than the development office, the president's office, or general administrators.

A key example takes us to Vermont. Along with his two brothers Jim and Remo, Angelo Pizzagalli provides the funding for the Pizzagalli Foundation based in Burlington. Angelo and his brothers learned to be masons from their father and built up a substantial real-estate and construction company. Specializing in sewer and water-treatment plants, theirs became the largest construction company in the Green Mountain State.

Because Angelo and Jim are University of Vermont alumni, they were no strangers to that school's culture. "Vermont is a very liberal place, and we felt that so many students were hearing only one side of many issues," Angelo told one interviewer. "Capitalism, free enterprise, and limited government...are not well understood on college campuses today." Concerned that such understanding was lacking at the University of Vermont, and with careful consideration to how they might best structure their giving, the brothers made a $3 million grant in 2017 to endow the Pizzagalli Chair of Free Enterprise at UVM's Grossman School of Business.

Community colleges train half of all students who pursue higher education, and are crucial to local economies. They tend to be very receptive to donors.

In crafting the six-page grant agreement for the endowed chair, the Pizzagalli Foundation worked closely with the Fund for Academic Renewal at the American Council of Trustees and Alumni (ACTA), which advises donors on best practices in higher-education philanthropy to promote adherence to donor intent. The agreement lays out the desired outcomes for the professorship and includes an escape clause that allows the Pizzagalli brothers to claw back their funding if the university goes astray. Additionally, the professorship is not endowed in perpetuity—it sunsets by 2049. The family members who reside in Burlington maintain a close relationship with UVM and can see for themselves how the institution is administering their grant. When Andrey Ukhov was installed as the first Pizzagalli Professor of Free Enterprise in April 2019, Angelo Pizzagalli was on hand to congratulate him.

Establishing named professorships in specific areas of study is a popular giving choice for college and university donors, as are scholarships and fellowships. Phoenix homebuilder Tom Lewis was introduced to Barrett, the residential honors college at Arizona State University. Highly selective and highly regarded, Barrett recruits outstanding students from across the United States. Lewis became more personally acquainted with Barrett when he and his wife Jan began funding 10 scholarships each year for Arizona freshmen entering the college. In addition to tuition, the awards included career counseling and personal development opportunities.

Lewis's philanthropy at ASU sparked his thinking about bringing a comprehensive honors college to the University of Kentucky, where he graduated with a degree in mechanical engineering in 1971. Lewis spent two full years in discussions with the university's president, head of development, and a specially appointed advisory board, mulling the mission and goals of the proposed new honors college. Only when he was sure that every key person was on board did Lewis commit $23 million to create U.K.'s Lewis Honors College and its Center for Personal Development.

After both of financier Paul Singer's sons attended Williams College, he was solicited by its development office for a large gift to a capital campaign. He declined that request and sought advice from trusted colleagues about ways to ensure that any support he did provide would be used wisely in areas he cared about. They cautioned him not to give endowment funds, but rather offer a couple years of funding at a time, renewable if used to his satisfaction, for specific purposes. They also recommended that he avoid going through the president or development head, but instead find a like-minded professor who would supervise all spending and program execution.

Singer identified Williams political scientist James McAllister as the person to create, with his donation, a new program in American foreign policy. For about $150,000 a year, the result is a lecture series, a visiting professor, a postdoctoral scholar, a journal, summer seminars, campus events, and a core group of 15 to 20 students at a time focused on strengthening America's position in the world. Singer notes that this amount of money would have been insignificant in a generalized capital campaign. But by defining his gift carefully, making it time-limited, repeatedly renewed, and run by a person whom he trusts, it has had real influence. The program is entering its twelfth year.

Higher-education donors have also opted to fund academic centers at colleges and universities, either by creating them from scratch or sustaining existing ones. The Charles Koch Foundation has supported well over 100 such centers focused on economic freedom, criminal justice and policing reform, tolerance and free expression, foreign policy, and technology and innovation. Examples of Koch Foundation investments include the Center for the History of Political Economy at Duke University, the Smith Institute for Political Economy and Philosophy at Chapman University, the Center for Grand Strategy within the Bush School of Government and Public Service at Texas A&M, and the Center for the Science of Moral Understanding at the University of North Carolina at Chapel Hill.

In 2018, the Koch Foundation made the decision to make all its multi-year grant agreements with major universities publicly available. Many such agreements, signed between 2016 and 2019, are now readable on the foundation's website. Donors considering funding new academic centers may find these grant agreements quite helpful in structuring their conversations with university leadership, faculty, and staff. All begin with a firm statement of support for "open inquiry and a diversity of ideas in higher education" and then include critical details that donors should not overlook. As an example, the agreement for a grant to the Arizona State University Foundation— supporting the Academy for Justice at the Sandra Day O'Connor College of Law—lays out the specific positions to be funded, the grant award schedule, and the conditions under which the donor has the right to terminate the award.

Adam Kissel, director of civic- and higher-education programs at the Philanthropy Roundtable, provides several considerations for donors interested in creating academic centers. These grow out of his experience directing gifts to higher education at the Charles Koch Foundation and the Jack Miller Center.

- Find a strong (ideally tenured) faculty member with both academic and administrative skills who shares your commitment to the proposed center's mission, and build the program around him or her. "It needs to be someone with an entrepreneurial vision, gravitas with his colleagues, and demonstrated ability to get the job done—not just someone who is a good scholar," Kissel advises.

- Ensure that the center lives within a department and will play an important role in the university's academic life. A significant risk is that a center will be isolated and languish in a remote corner of the institution.
- Involve other faculty members and trustees as partners early in the process.
- Make sure that any new permanent faculty brought into the center are full members of the department in which the center is housed. Equip the center to bring in visiting faculty to enhance the center's research and teaching potential.
- Ensure that the institution's development office will give the new center necessary assistance.
- Ensure that top administration leaders, right up to the president, respect academic freedom, particularly if you are launching a more controversial center, such as one centered around free markets or free expression.
- Always allocate your funding in a year-to-year arrangement. Academic and administrative personnel will certainly change, and future arrivals may not share your interests.
- Ensure that the center allows for diversity of thought and opinion, which on most campuses means protecting right-of-center viewpoints that are grossly underrepresented. Two good models: Professor Robert George's Madison Program at Princeton University, and Professor John Tomasi's Political Theory Project at Brown University whose student wing, the Janus Forum, brings to campus thinkers of various ideological stripes to debate issues.

Depending on mission, higher-education donors would also be wise to consider investments in institutions outside the usual circuit of well-known liberal-arts colleges and research universities granting baccalaureate and advanced degrees. It's easy to forget that community colleges train half of all the students who pursue higher education, and that they are often crucial to improving local economies. Trade and technical schools are even more overlooked, but also crucial to the success of our businesses and culture. These institutions tend to be very receptive to donors with creative ideas about skill training and upward mobility in America.

Consider the example of donor Karen Wright, CEO of the gas-compressor manufacturer Ariel Corporation. Wright has invested millions in community colleges and trade schools in central Ohio, including

When donors demand accountability

Philanthropists sometimes find themselves demanding accountability from a university for more than their own grants. This was the case in September 2016 when the James Graham Brown Foundation warned the University of Louisville that it would halt its giving to the university—which amounted to more than $74 million in grants since 1954—until university leaders conducted a forensic audit of the University of Louisville Foundation.

James Graham Brown was a lumberman, horseman, and entrepreneur who built his fortune through construction sales and real-estate development in Louisville in the early-to-mid twentieth century. He turned to philanthropy with the goal of improving the public image of Kentucky as a state and Louisville as a city. He helped to establish the Louisville Zoo and expand the footprint of the University of Louisville. In the 1970s and 1980s, his foundation began to fund chairs, endowments, and professorships at the university. It provided the first of many grants to establish a first-class regional cancer center under the university's direction.

Concerns about the center's progress in the late 2000s led the foundation to begin asking questions about the grants it had made for that purpose. The answers were not forthcoming. "It was absolutely confusing every time someone tried to explain how our money was being used," says Mason Rummel, president of the James Graham Brown Foundation. In response, the Brown Foundation and another University of Louisville supporter—the C. E. and S. Foundation—demanded a forensic audit of the University of Louisville Foundation, which they paid for with a combined gift of $2 million. The audit revealed a series of questionable loans, bad investments, unauthorized compensation schemes, and numerous unbudgeted transactions that had never been disclosed to the university foundation's board members. "It was toxic and convoluted," remarks Rummel. "The audit met our worst expectations, but there was some sense of relief to know that our suspicions weren't crazy."

Initially concerned that a grantee was ignoring the stated purpose of one of its own gifts, the foundation found itself assuming the role of watchdog, whistleblower, and reformer of a much broader pattern of financial malfeasance. Ongoing donor oversight is crucial in higher-education giving.

Stark State, Central Ohio Technical College, Zane State, and the Knox County Career Center. Wright's contributions helped create a Career and Technical Education curriculum that shepherds graduates into well-paying jobs without the need for a four-year degree.

North Carolina donor Penny Enroth of the Palmer Foundation has invested over $500,000 in building a trades instruction facility at Sandhills Community College. This offers students credentials in production technology, electrical contracting, advanced welding, and other vocations that our economy desperately needs today. Students end up highly employable. And college administrators are respectful of donor intent.

Guidance for effective grantmaking in higher education

Despite the steep challenges, donors who are committed to supporting higher education need not shy away. America needs wise philanthropists who invest judiciously in this area. So how can you give while protecting your donor intent?

Be crystal clear in your personal conversations and grant agreements
Don't assume colleges and universities understand or share your goals. Amir Pasic, dean of the Lilly Family School of Philanthropy at Indiana University, notes that "crafting the gift agreement to reflect the donor's intent, and describing how the organization plans to use the gift, is vital." But remember that even the best gift agreement can only go so far. The real work is accomplished by building strong relationships with the key faculty and administrators responsible for implementing the project you want to fund. Reaching agreement with university representatives about the details of your donation, and then requesting that they include all the agreed-on terms in their final proposal to you, makes the shared obligations obvious to all parties.

A complete gift agreement should include the amount of your gift, how and when it will be paid, a clear statement of purpose, a description of how—and on what timeline—the grantee will fulfill that purpose, your reporting requirements, the kind of involvement you would like to have in the funded program (e.g., meeting scholarship recipients, seeing supported papers and research, etc.), the conditions under which your grant will be renewable (if appropriate), and the circumstances which will lead to termination. You should always include a contingency plan that provides for a different—and specific—use of your funds in clearly defined situations, requires the institution to request permission from you or a designated representative before a grant is "repurposed," and a reversion clause whereby a gift will be returned to the donor if a grantee fails to adhere with restrictions in the original grant agreement.

While the terms "gift" and "grant" are used interchangeably in practice (and in this guidebook), it is advisable for individual donors to use the term "grant" for all higher-ed donations that include binding terms. Research universities in particular make a distinction between "gifts"—which are deemed irrevocable, unrestricted, and free of donor expectations—and "grants" for which donors have prescribed a precise scope of work to be performed in a specified time period.

Don't accept a grant agreement from a university
These documents are designed to protect the university's interests, not your own. Drawing up an original agreement is well worth the time and expense. While there are excellent university development officers who are careful to tease out a donor's ultimate intentions, you should independently delineate precisely what your philanthropic goals are. "People who don't have goals get used by people who do," warns Lewis. "If you don't have goals as a donor, you're easy prey."

Never waive your right to a *cy pres* review by the courts in a grant agreement. In many instances, universities automatically include a clause essentially banning a third-party arbiter (such as the state's attorney general or a court) from stepping in to mediate should a donor-intent dispute arise. Look for language in a grant agreement stipulating that if it becomes "illegal, impossible, impractical, or wasteful" to continue as is, the university is free to change the grant agreement however it wishes. "I strike this language every time I see it," notes philanthropic consultant Fred Fransen. "I then substitute my own wording, emphasizing donor rights. To date, no university has ever insisted on restoring the original language. It seems that universities recognize that they have no moral right to take advantage of donor generosity, or inexperience."

Don't hesitate to ask lots of questions, even in later stages of the process
"Higher-education philanthropy is so incredibly complex," says Mason Rummel. "Recognize that. Don't assume there are any dumb questions. If you have a question, ask it. Don't hold back because no one else is asking it." Donors to public institutions should understand clearly the relationship between the university and the university's foundation.

Donors to all colleges should understand how indirect costs are assessed, and develop written policies to address them. Some donors refuse to cover any indirect costs. Others, including the Gates and Templeton Foundations, cap their coverage at a maximum rate.

Avoid the traps of unrestricted and endowment grantmaking
While unrestricted gifts could make sense in other philanthropic realms—particularly for recipients with whom you have a close working relationship—they are fraught with peril in the realm of higher education. Know that your philanthropic dollars are easily shifted around at colleges, and that if you object they have lots of lawyers who will respond. Giving officers often steer donors toward unrestricted gifts precisely because they offer maximum flexibility to the recipient institution. Unless you are very specific with your

> Unrestricted gifts that might make sense for other recipients are fraught with peril in the realm of higher education.

desires, and write them out, your gifts could be used for something you find abhorrent. Jim Piereson recommends that "Rather than writing open-ended checks, donors should target their contributions in ways that allow them to designate the programs and professors they wish to support."

Endowment gifts are equally problematic for donor intent: "There is no way to ensure proper use for all eternity," wrote Jerry Martin and Anne Neal in their essay, "Questions to Ask Before You Write the Check to Higher Education." Once a donor is out of the picture—through either death or disinterest—funds may be mismanaged or deliberately diverted to purposes other than those originally specified. Endowing a professorship in perpetuity, Fransen reminds donors, fails to consider the possibility that a field of study may become far less popular or relevant over time or that "the next professor...may have an entirely different agenda." Piereson notes that such gifts are also inefficient. Shorter-term gifts will have greater impact than those which "pay out just 5 percent of their value on an annual basis."

Create a funding stream rather than a lump-sum gift
Donor intent and accountability are best served by grants made in increments over a limited term, with continued donations dependent on
scheduled progress reports. "I learned the hard way to focus my philanthropic investing, give annualized grants, and demand detailed reporting," notes Jack Miller. You could, for example, structure a $10 million
grant for a new program over a 10-year period: first provide $3 million
to enable the university to hire personnel and create the necessary infra-
structure. But schedule the remaining $7 million in regular payments,
periodically reviewing to ensure the school is on track. "Start small and

For college gifts, accountability is best served
by grants made in increments over a
limited time, with continuation
dependent on progress reports.

start short," Lewis suggests. If one of his foundation's grantees fails to
make adequate progress toward stated goals, Lewis has the right to terminate the agreement and halt all further payments.

Create an independent nonprofit
Donors have also created institutes informally connected to—but
administratively and financially independent from—institutions of higher education. Founded in 2003 by individuals associated with Princeton
University's James Madison Program and several national foundations,
the Witherspoon Institute is one such nonprofit. Its proximity to the
Princeton campus allows it to draw on Princeton's faculty expertise
and offer occasional events in collaboration with university depart-
ments and programs. But Witherspoon has ample resources to operate its own research and education programs, and the institute offers
higher-education donors a distinct financial bonus: grants made through
Witherspoon to support faculty members at Princeton or other universities with which the institute is collaborating limit any overhead charge
to 10 percent. The Foundation for Excellence in Higher Education
assists in supporting such independent institutes, among them the Abigail
Adams Institute (Harvard), Houston Institute (Rice), Zephyr Institute
(Stanford), and Elm Institute (Yale).

Give through an intermediary funder and/or designate a contingent beneficiary

An intermediary funder might be a mission-driven donor-advised fund sponsor such as DonorsTrust, National Christian Foundation, or—for left-leaning donors—Tides Foundation. You might also consider a trusted charity that shares your principles and with whom you have an established relationship. Giving to a college or university through an intermediary is a good choice for higher-education donors who lack the time, expertise, or inclination to monitor and administer a complex, multi-year grant agreement. An intermediary can assist you in defining your intentions, evaluating potential grantees, brokering the relationship between you and your grantee, monitoring compliance with grant terms, and making payments on a defined schedule.

You may also consider naming a contingent beneficiary with standing to sue if your original grantee fails to follow your wishes. Acting as a contingent beneficiary, Hillsdale College brought a 2017 suit against the University of Missouri alleging misuse of a $5 million endowment left to U.M. by Sherlock Hibbs in 2002. He stipulated his gift was to create six professorships filled by disciples of the Ludwig von Mises school of economics, and that if the school failed to respect the terms of his grant the money should shift to Hillsdale instead. When the professors hired to date failed to meet Hibbs's standard, Hillsdale College sued Missouri on the donor's behalf. In 2019 the two institutions announced that they had reached a settlement stipulating that Hillsdale will receive $4.6 million—half of the remaining endowment, and the University of Missouri will hold a symposium focused on Austrian economics at least every two years. Hibbs's decision to name a contingent beneficiary to monitor the original grantee (and take legal action if needed) thus limited further erosion of his legacy gift.

Give while you're living

It may seem cynical to assume that institutions pay more attention to living donors, but it is true that mischief in higher-education philanthropy often occurs after a donor's death. College faculty and administrators are more likely to discover new "pressing" needs that outweigh the instructions of the original benefactor once that person is no longer in the picture. The solution is simple: do your giving while you're alive—when you can personally assess the best opportunities, form relationships with administrators and staff, make the investments, monitor performance, and reevaluate your decisions as needed. Giving while living also gives you the unique chance to have an outsized influence through larger gift amounts, and it brings you more joy to see for yourself the impact of your philanthropy.

Shop your proposal to multiple institutions
Higher-education donors frequently focus on their alma maters, which may not be the best institutions for the programs they are considering. In these instances, donors are likely to encounter administrators who persuade them to modify their gifts to suit institutional priorities. "Don't focus on just one university," advises Fransen. "The dynamics of the negotiation are different if there are multiple options on the table. These conversations, when you're shopping, are very revelatory about which schools are interested and which just want your money."

If you push an unenthusiastic institution to accept your gift and your terms—especially if you are paying for the entire undertaking yourself—you will most likely be dissatisfied with the half-hearted effort that results. One acid test for whether a university is truly on board is to require joint funding, i.e., an arrangement where the university commits its own funds to the project as well. Tom Lewis strives to do this with all his higher-education grantmaking.

Find faculty and administration friends, and form relationships
Success in higher-education giving requires forming trusted relationships with individuals within the university. Most important, look for friendly faculty members who can advance your ideas internally. They are the most critical players—they will execute your project and are the ones most likely to serve as guardians of your donor intent because you share the same goals. At the same time, remember that faculty members may leave or be reassigned. Tenured faculty are less prone to switching institutions, but it does happen. Any unwritten understandings you had with an individual will be forgotten when personnel changes, Fransen warns. So cultivate relationships with deans, provosts, college presidents, and trustees to build more support and continuity for your project.

Respect academic freedom
The wishes of donors are sometimes at odds with academic freedom. While you have every right to bring your own values to your

philanthropy and fund only those faculty members and programs that align with those values, you cannot interfere with internal academic processes. As Martin and Neal noted, "You will not be permitted to appoint faculty, prescribe reading lists, or determine which courses are required." You may define a broad subject area—American political history or free enterprise, for example—but you cannot dictate the actual curriculum. Generally, well-endowed universities will refuse to allow any donor involvement in the selection and approval process for academic appointments. In some instances, however, donors have been permitted to attend selection committee meetings and/or have a voice in the final decision among candidates that have been deemed qualified by others. This is a matter that a donor must discuss with the recipient institution during the development of the grant agreement. In all cases donors may wish to consider using a version of the statement now included in Koch Foundation "center" grant agreements to make its position on academic freedom both clear and transparent:

> Consistent with the Donor's principles of supporting open inquiry and a diversity of ideas in higher education, the Donor's grant is intended to help promote a republic of science at the University where ideas can be exchanged freely and useful knowledge will benefit the well-being of individuals and society. Thus, the Parties agree that the academic freedom of the University, the Center and their faculty, students, and staff is critical to the success of the Center's research, scholarship, teaching, and service.

Be patient

A natural tension exists between the instincts of donors—frequently business-savvy men and women with an entrepreneurial streak, accustomed to moving quickly and having their orders obeyed—and the glacial process of academic procedures. Moreover, the shared governance structure in higher education—where a board of trustees or faculty senate may have a say in a university's grant proposal and its gift acceptance—can cause added frustrations. The best course forward is to take your time, trust your relationships, and avoid trying to micromanage the process. A solid gift agreement may involve multiple conversations and a great deal of editing. Recall that Lewis spent two years in discussions with multiple persons at the University of Kentucky before he committed his gift to establish an honors college.

Consider less-typical gifts and institutions
Academic centers, buildings, professorships, and scholarships are the staples of higher-education giving and will always be popular choices for donors. But look more broadly at the possibilities. Gifts that support independent study and leadership development among students can have potent effects on individuals. Gifts that support graduate students committed to individual liberty, the rule of law, and economic freedom can alter the ideological profile of the future professoriate. Gifts that promote debate—whether student or faculty directed—can bring new and different points of view to a campus and change its level of intellectual diversity and free speech. If campus intolerance is a special concern, you might follow the example of the John W. Altman Charitable Foundation, which now makes adoption of the University of Chicago Principles of Freedom of Expression a condition for all its higher-education philanthropy. "Giving to higher ed doesn't have to be directed to an institution or to putting a name on a building," says Jack Miller. "Who knows what that institution will be doing or how that building will be used in 50 years? Better to sponsor annual programming on campus that teaches values you believe in."

> Giving to colleges through an intermediary
> is a good choice for donors who lack the time,
> expertise, or inclination to monitor.

Look beyond the elite four-year colleges and universities to find high-performing community colleges, trade schools, technical institutes, local colleges, and online programs where your gifts can have great impact. Many of these institutions are on the cutting edge of economic progress, and make important contributions to regional prosperity through workforce development and upskilling programs. Community colleges, in particular, offer one of today's most underutilized investment opportunities for higher-education funders.

Seek advice from trusted sources
When you read the dire stories of infringed donor intent it is easy to get discouraged, especially in higher-education philanthropy. But there are

excellent resources available to advise donors in this area. They include faculty members directing campus programs that honor donor intent, private consultants, funders who have successfully navigated the hazards, and nonprofit organizations such as DonorsTrust, the Fund for Academic Renewal, the Institute for Humane Studies, the Jack Miller Center for Teaching America's Founding Principles and History, and The Philanthropy Roundtable. If you are looking for a worthwhile program at your alma mater or elsewhere and have questions about specific issues like free speech on campus, or developing your grant agreement, you can reach out to a trusted source at any point in the process for information and guidance on defining and securing your charitable intentions.

Recovering Donor Intent
When Things Go Wrong

The best defense against a breach of your intentions as a donor is to take proactive steps: create a strong mission statement, populate your board with people you trust, time-limit your foundation, and establish internal and external accountability mechanisms. In the best of circumstances, you, your heirs, and your successor trustees will never experience a donor-intent crisis. But if one does occur, what should you do? This chapter shares the stories of three philanthropies—the Daniels Fund, Atlantic Philanthropies, and the Triad Foundation—and extracts lessons that you as a donor can use to recover your philanthropy's mission, should a violation arise.

Building on the bedrock of a donor's principles: Daniels Fund
Once a foundation veers off course from a donor's original intent, it's rare that a full-fledged return to that intent occurs. But that's what happened on the Colorado front range in the early 2000s. Trustees at the Daniels Fund led a systematic process to restore and protect grantmaking based on the donor's core values.

Born in 1920 in Colorado, Bill Daniels grew up in New Mexico. Scrappy from an early age, he won two state Golden Gloves boxing championships in high school, then served as a U.S. Navy fighter pilot in both World War II and the Korean War. Daniels moved to Casper, Wyoming, in 1952. Intrigued by television and amazed by its growing popularity, Daniels was dismayed that its signals could not reach mountain towns like Casper. As a workaround, Daniels invested in coaxial cable and secured 4,000 subscribing households (about a third of the total homes in the area). His business took off from there. The cable television boom of the 1980s and 1990s made Daniels very wealthy.

Throughout his life, his charitable giving ranged widely. He reached out to those down on their luck, those who abused alcohol and drugs, and those who suffered from mental and physical disabilities. He provided scholarships, with a focus less on academic achievement and more on demonstrated character and leadership potential. He funded efforts to integrate ethics into business schools, and created a bank meant to teach young people the principles of finance and personal responsibility. Through it all, his giving was largely personal: Daniels routinely enclosed a note with each check, explaining to the recipient what he hoped his money would do.

When Daniels passed away in 2000, his estate transferred to the Daniels Fund, making it one of the largest foundations in the nation. Even though he believed he had clearly codified his donor intent—delineating which geographic areas and causes he wished to support and which he didn't, and even listing funding amounts for his favorites—he had failed to clarify the underlying values and principles that should guide the foundation's giving. That omission, combined with professional staff whose worldviews differed from the donor's, produced a culture unfriendly to Daniels' original vision.

"They were good people, but they didn't know Bill," notes Linda Childears, who was one of the first seven board members of the Daniels Fund. "They didn't have his experiences and so they didn't think like him." This was typified in 2002 when a staff member turned down a grant request from the Smithsonian National Air and Space Museum to fund an educational exhibit featuring World War II aircraft—on the grounds that it would be inappropriate to fund a project featuring "instruments of war." When it was pointed out that Daniels himself had piloted the same type of aircraft to defend the cause of freedom, the program officer still insisted that the request be declined.

That incident was "a wake-up call," says John Saeman, a member of the Daniels Fund board at the time who later served as chairman. "Suddenly the Daniels Fund was starting to look like someone else's foundation," summarizes Childears. Daniels' original donor intent was being disregarded, prompting a majority of the board to intervene. The result was a five-year effort to ensure that Bill Daniels' intentions and ideals would underpin the way the foundation conducted its business.

The first major step was to consolidate staffing by closing regional offices across the Mountain West, to prevent the Daniels Fund from becoming a behemoth with many heads. An analysis also showed the organization was spending about 20 percent more on administrative overhead than its peer foundations, in large part because of the satellite offices.

Next came the codification of Daniels' intent in writing. Directors pored over their founder's letters and writings. They carefully studied his giving history—Daniels had made charitable gifts for 25 years prior to his death—and interviewed numerous associates to better understand his intentions. After careful deliberation the directors defined grant areas, guidelines, and grantmaking parameters, all anchored in Daniels' words and deeds. They amended the foundation's bylaws to include these new donor-intent documents—including ones that told Daniels' story from beginning to end, creating a fuller profile of the man that left no doubt about his values and principles. Then the board stipulated that a 90 percent majority of the board would be required to amend the Daniels Fund giving parameters in the future.

Today the Daniels Fund focuses on grantmaking in areas closely in line with Bill Daniels' wishes and history, including aid for the down-and-out, help for those addicted to drugs and alcohol, and college scholarships for hundreds of students every year as they graduate from high schools in Colorado, New Mexico, Utah, and Wyoming. The foundation could easily have taken a wholly different direction were it not for the intervention of alert trustees and loyal friends.

The moral authority of a living donor: Atlantic Philanthropies
At the core of the donor-intent dispute that unfolded at Atlantic Philanthropies between 2009 and 2012 was one key question: "What deference does an independent board owe to the moral—if not legal—authority of a living donor?" Unlike so many other donor-intent tales, this was a conflict in which the donor himself, Chuck Feeney, was able to express his dissatisfaction directly to the board and staff with whom he disagreed.

By 2009, Atlantic Philanthropies had been operating for over 25 years and had allocated significant sums of money for charitable purposes. Beginning with a focus on American higher education (particularly at Feeney's alma mater, Cornell University), Atlantic had become a global funder of social change in aging, education, health, and human rights. Because the philanthropy had been incorporated in Bermuda, it was not subject to the restrictions placed on 501c3 organizations in the United States. As a result, Atlantic had the ability to support not only traditional nonprofit organizations, but also political causes. Feeney fully supported Atlantic's focus on the disadvantaged, but a growing dissatisfaction with staff and board decisions pulling the group more and more into politics eventually led to his personal intervention to reorient the foundation to the priorities and strategies he deemed best.

> The interests, values, and passions
> of the donor should be given
> central consideration in spending
> the fruits of his labor.

As described in Conor O'Clery's *The Billionaire Who Wasn't: How Chuck Feeney Secretly Made and Gave Away a Fortune* (a biography which Feeney authorized), the crisis at Atlantic Philanthropies began in 2009. Atlantic's endowment at that time was $3 billion. Two years prior, Gara LaMarche had been appointed president of Atlantic, after serving at George Soros's Open Society Institute. Despite some warning signs that LaMarche would favor left-wing giving to a larger degree, Feeney joined the rest of the board in approving the hire.

At the same time, Feeney was growing increasingly distant from Atlantic's other board members. His original trustees of the 1980s, all personal friends or professional colleagues, were long gone, with only one exception. Staff members had also lost close contact with him as Atlantic operated from multiple offices around the world and Feeney himself was spending far less time in New York City. Then the election of Barack Obama to the Presidency in 2008—a victory which Feeney celebrated—gave LaMarche and his supporters even more leeway to pursue a costly "social-justice" agenda. For example, Atlantic invested $26.5 million in an advocacy campaign to pass the Affordable Care Act. Leaders of the Obamacare effort later said that, "Without Gara and Atlantic, the United States would not have enacted this legislation."

Feeney was not opposed to improving access to health care, but didn't believe that political activism was the most effective application of his charitable funds. In seeking "the highest and best use" for Atlantic's assets, Feeney saw far better outcomes from the capital projects that had always appealed to his entrepreneurial inclination to give talented people great places to work.

Feeney was also growing increasingly uneasy about Atlantic's new style and level of operations. LaMarche had developed a high visibility nationally, being invited to the White House for the signing of the Affordable Care Act. This was in stark contrast to Feeney's preferred approach of quiet and unassuming, anonymous philanthropy. The CEO had also initiated a move of the foundation's offices from 24,000 square feet of space to 44,000 square feet, a decision that cost nearly $19 million.

Due to the way Atlantic Philanthropies had developed its governance structure over the years, Feeney was only one of 12 votes on the board. In a 2009 letter to the board he expressed his displeasure with the general direction of the foundation under LaMarche's leadership. He particularly objected to the overtly political "social-justice" spending that was edging out other projects close to his philanthropic heart. His pleas fell on deaf ears.

Eventually, Feeney called for the resignation of three board members whom he saw as siding with LaMarche to too great a degree. They refused. Feeney says one told him, "You will have to carry me out on a stretcher."

Adding to Feeney's consternation, there was increasing debate and concern about whether the board would sunset the foundation by 2016, as the board had agreed in 2002. There was argument over whether the funds should still be considered "Feeney's money." "Underlying everything was the question of whether the directors had the right and the duty to determine how it should be put to use, regardless of the donor's priorities," writes O'Clery in his book.

In September 2010 Feeney sent a 2,000-word "manifesto" to each board member outlining his concerns and objections. He said he disagreed with the "social-justice" approach, that Atlantic Philanthropy's recent grantmaking was not what he had in mind when he set up the endowment, and that it was not something he could support. He again requested that the three board members resign, along with LaMarche. He proposed that all grantmaking be halted for a reset.

Feeney urged "a moral and fiduciary obligation that the interests, values, and passions of the living sole donor be given central consideration in spending the fruits of his labor." In response, the board retained legal counsel on the question of Feeney's rights, further outraging the donor by spending hundreds of thousands of dollars on legal fees. As the situation spiraled further out of control, an anonymous writer claiming to represent a group of Feeney's friends sent the board a letter threatening to take the conflict public.

"What will potential philanthropists think if they find out that a foundation board doesn't listen to the wishes of the founder when he is alive and sitting in the room, never mind when he is dead?" The board also received another missive, this one from nine staff members, questioning recent decisions on operations and grantmaking at Atlantic. The staff letter reinforced the determination of the minority of board members sympathetic to Feeney.

In mid-2011, LaMarche finally resigned, as did the board's chairman less than a month later. Feeney himself resigned from the board and his longtime friend and trusted associate Chris Oechsli took over as president. Oechsli proceeded to initiate a review of grantmaking with the goal of refocusing on four core grant areas and the founder's programs. By the end of 2012, all the board members to whom Feeney had objected were gone, either resigned or disqualified by new term limits established for trustees.

The dispute at Atlantic Philanthropies provides the most dramatic example of a donor-intent crisis to date, because it happened while the living donor was still actively engaged. The absence of a clear and detailed statement of donor intent from Feeney, and the failure to create a governance structure that protected the prerogatives of the living donor, fueled this collision. See Chapter 5 for more on the special circumstances of living donors.

Recovering a legacy for the future: Triad Foundation

Imagine a pot of money that supports both the liberal Media Matters and the conservative Media Research Center. Both the Center for Public Integrity and the Heritage Foundation. Both *Mother Jones* and *National Review.* That describes the fortune earned by media executive and businessman Roy Hampton Park, known as the founder of the Duncan Hines line of packaged foods and a pioneer in the world of newspapers, broadcasting, and mass communications. Today Park's money supports two separate family foundations based in Ithaca, New York. The story of the split of his legacy into the Park Foundation and Triad Foundation offers a final example, for this chapter on recovering donor intent, of how things can go wrong.

> It was heartbreaking to see
> what my father worked so hard to make
> being directed to grants
> unrelated to what he believed.

Roy Park was a determined, individualistic entrepreneur—a self-made man in the truest sense. He created the Park Foundation in 1966 and gave generously to educational, religious, and other charitable organizations in his home community of Ithaca and in other locales where he owned media outlets. Park passed away in 1993, by which time Park Communications had acquired or created 22 radio stations, 11 television stations, and 144 publications, including 42 newspapers. With an infusion of most of the $711 million from his company's sale in the mid-1990s, the Park Foundation transformed very suddenly from a modest, corporate-oriented foundation run primarily by the donor and his spouse into a significantly larger family foundation with a board composed of both family and non-family members.

The Park Foundation trustees agreed on certain aspects of Roy Park's legacy, which allowed them to establish, in 1996, scholarship and fellowship programs at Cornell University, Ithaca College, North Carolina State University (his alma mater), and the University of North Carolina at Chapel Hill. However, Park's two children—Roy Park Jr. and Adelaide Park Gomer—sparred over the ideological direction of the foundation in the ensuing years. Park Jr. objected to funds used for environmental activism and other left-wing causes. "It was heartbreaking to see what my father worked so hard to make being directed to grants I felt were so unrelated to what he believed," Park Jr. says. The conflict came to a head in the fall of 2001, when Park's widow, Dorothy Park, proposed to split the foundation into two with separate boards. Dorothy and her daughter Adelaide continued to operate the now left-leaning Park Foundation, while her son Roy took the helm of the right-leaning Triad Foundation, with his son and daughter as his fellow directors.

Donor Roy Park's biggest misstep was leaving nothing in writing regarding his mission and intentions for his foundation. Like John Andrus, he may have assumed that his conservative and free-market beliefs could be easily deciphered from his work ethic and entrepreneurial nature, his political and religious preferences, his own track record of philanthropy, and the personal letters and public statements he left behind. But without explicit instructions, family members drew widely divergent conclusions. Today both his daughter and son maintain that they are following Park's donor intent, even though their philanthropic priorities are poles apart.

To reduce confusion heading into the future, and to strengthen donor intent at the Triad Foundation, Roy Park Jr. has written a legacy statement codifying his father's philanthropic values for future generations. It contains a statement of principles and a detailed philanthropic biography of his father—a concrete look into who the man was and what he believed, including ample direct quotes. It makes clear that Roy Park supported democracy and free enterprise, limited government, religious liberty, freedom of thought, and broad access to education and employment. It also contains a geographic restriction, focusing community-based grants on the areas where Triad Foundation family members live.

"Triad seeks to avoid the trend of most foundations established by free-enterprise entrepreneurs which almost inevitably, once the founders pass on, move firmly into the grip of orthodox liberalism," Park Jr. explains. In his book, *Sons in the Shadows*, Park Jr. is even more adamant: "My father's legacy is not one to be forgotten, and what he worked for all his life should not be ignored or refuted. I was sensitive to erosion of his hardworking lifetime ideals, and despite the absence of his intentions for the foundation's mission in his will, the philanthropic objectives that best reflected the interests of my side of the family were evident in the previous 30-year history of his grant making.... As far as my family was concerned, no one was going to trample on his grave."

Precautions for recovering your intent

Unfortunately, stories of successful recaptures of donor intent are rare. Far more prevalent are stories of permanent departure from a funder's original wishes. If you find yourself in a donor-intent crisis, or you aim to prevent one in the future, keep these guideposts in mind:

People make the difference

For the Daniels Fund, the key ingredients for recovery of donor intent were trustees and staff members unafraid to ruffle feathers in order to preserve the donor's original wishes. Childears recalls that when she assumed leadership, "I was stunned by how many professionals in philanthropy asked me, 'What new direction will you take at the Daniels Fund?' It simply never occurred to me that I would take the Daniels Fund in any direction other than the one defined by our donor. It seems commonplace for many of my peers in the foundation world to believe that fidelity to donor intent denies them the ability to respond creatively to the 'problems of today.' They have the right to their opinions, but they do not have the right to violate donor intent."

Be judicious about board governance

While you're living, it's advisable to view your board members as consultants, there to offer their expertise but ultimately to follow your wishes. Giving them too much power can be dangerous, as was the case at Atlantic Philanthropies, where Feeney was only one voting member. "While the donor is still alive, the board should serve in more of an advisory role than as a true governing board," suggests Al Mueller. "If you set it up where the board can outvote the donor, you've made a big mistake. When you pass away, they can then turn into an independent board of directors." You should, of course, balance this precaution with the need to grant enough authority and responsibility to board members to equip them with the knowledge and experience to carry on your philanthropy if you plan to sunset years after your death, or operate in perpetuity.

In situations where a donor failed to create a statement of intent, craft a legacy statement

Follow the example of Roy Park Jr. Tell the donor's life story and how it relates to his or her philanthropic intentions. Name the donor's core values and priorities and specify what should, and should not, be funded. Identify gifts made in the donor's lifetime and why they are meaningful. Use the donor's own words, drawn from correspondence or speeches, as much as possible.

CHAPTER

Conclusion

When it comes to preserving your philanthropic intent, perhaps Jerry Hume of the Jaquelin Hume Foundation says it best: "Donor beware." As we've explored in this guidebook, the pitfalls of donor intent are many. Here are the top ten mistakes that undermine donor intent:

1. Writing a vague and easily misinterpreted mission statement.
2. Failing to include an explanation of your underlying values and principles in your mission statement.
3. Ignoring the weaknesses of your chosen philanthropic vehicle.
4. Failing to establish a governance structure that supports

donor intent, and, for living donors, not clarifying what role you will play in decisionmaking.

5. Bringing on board members and staff who don't respect your values and principles and/or view the resources of your charitable vehicle as their own.

6. Failing to work closely with your board members to help them understand not only your giving preferences, but also your philosophical outlook and your preferred grantmaking strategies and charitable targets.

7. Establishing a foundation in perpetuity without policies and procedures to protect donor intent. Opening a donor-advised fund without naming successor advisers who share your values and principles and without adding a sunset provision.

8. Failing to establish a review process for board members and a removal process for those who are not faithful to your intent.

9. Creating a family foundation or family donor-advised fund without acknowledging that radical differences and few shared values among family members are a common occurence.

10. Making endowment gifts to charities without establishing clear guidelines on their use.

These errors and omissions can undermine your donor intent both in the present and the future. But there are steps you can take that will dramatically increase the likelihood of your intent being honored:

- Define your charitable mission clearly in writing. Consider adding audio and/or video so future trustees and staff have a more personal perspective.
- Bring in legal representation to protect your intentions and stay abreast of nonprofit law and tax policy.
- Add your intentions to your articles of incorporation and bylaws.
- Choose trustees and staff who share your deepest principles and goals for your philanthropy. Consider having them affirm their commitment to donor intent in writing.
- Clarify your board design, and consider a tiered governance structure.
- Implement board policies that strengthen donor intent.
- Avoid mixing your philanthropic goals with corporate interests. Keep your corporate giving separate from your foundation to

ensure that company practices (e.g., giving in all communities where the business operates, or matching employee charitable gifts) don't dilute your personal intent.

- Clarify the role you want family members to play in your philanthropy, recognizing the many potentially negative impacts of family dynamics on governance and mission.
- If you are planning to utilize outside experts in your field of philanthropy, then clarify what role they will play.
- Consider giving while living or sunsetting your foundation. If you choose to operate a foundation in perpetuity, install the guardrails discussed in this guidebook as a protective measure.
- Incorporate your mission, vision, and values into the operations and culture of your philanthropy.
- Create internal and external policies to reinforce your intent.
- Strike the right balance between specificity and rigidity for those who will succeed you in your philanthropy to avoid having your donor intent deemed unfeasible and subject to a *cy pres* determination in court.

Above all, recognize that protecting your donor intent is your responsibility. Philanthropy observer Waldemar Nielsen once noted, "If a donor simply abandons a fortune to a piece of paper and the whole thing subsequently goes sour, the donor just can't complain about the lawyer's faulty advice or about careless preparation." Your success in philanthropy rests on your commitment to do the hard thinking about your donor intent, and then to build the best structure with the best people to fulfill your mission.

ACKNOWLEDGMENTS

Thanks are due to the many people who made this guidebook possible.

To all those who have so generously supported our philanthropic services program, and especially to the Daniels Fund, the Triad Foundation, the T. W. Lewis Foundation, and the Sunderland Foundation for their gifts in support of this guidebook.

To the donors, foundation leaders, and philanthropic advisers who shared their experiences and wisdom in interviews, and responded to my continued questions.

To Jeffrey Cain and Paul Rhoads, whose earlier guidebooks on donor intent formed a solid and helpful basis for this work.

To Philanthropy Roundtable colleague David Riggs, Andras Kosaras and Cara Koss of Arnold and Porter, Matthew Elkins and Alexander Reid of Morgan Lewis, Daniel Stuart of Marcus and Shapira, and Lawson Bader of DonorsTrust for their invaluable assistance with the discussion of philanthropic vehicles.

To the Roundtable's publications team, whose superb editing and graphic design helped make this guidebook a reader-friendly tool for all who use it.

To Adam Meyerson, who read every word of this guidebook over several iterations and improved it each time with his insightful questions and observations.

To expert readers Kim Dennis and Jim Piereson, who gave graciously of their time, thoughtfulness, and encouragement.

And to David Bass, whose outstanding work in conducting over 30 interviews, researching the many aspects of donor intent, and preparing a first draft is evident on every page of this guidebook.

Joanne Florino
Vice president, philanthropic services, The Philanthropy Roundtable

INDEX

ABOUT THE PHILANTHROPY ROUNDTABLE

The Philanthropy Roundtable is America's leading network of charitable donors working to strengthen our free society, uphold donor intent, and protect the freedom to give. Our members include individual philanthropists, families, corporations, and private foundations.

Mission

The Philanthropy Roundtable's mission is to foster excellence in philanthropy, to protect philanthropic freedom, to assist donors in achieving their philanthropic intent, and to help donors advance liberty, opportunity, and personal responsibility in America and abroad.

Principles

- Philanthropic freedom is essential to a free society.
- A vibrant private sector generates the wealth that makes philanthropy possible.
- Voluntary private action offers solutions to many of society's most pressing challenges.
- Excellence in philanthropy is measured by results, not by good intentions.
- A respect for donor intent is essential to long-term philanthropic success.

Services

World-class conferences

The Philanthropy Roundtable connects you with other savvy donors. Held across the nation throughout the year, our meetings assemble grantmakers and experts to develop strategies for excellent local, state, and national giving. You will hear from innovators in K-12 education, economic opportunity, higher education, national security, and other fields. Our Annual Meeting is the Roundtable's flagship event, gathering the nation's most public-spirited and influential philanthropists for debates, how-to sessions, and discussions on the best ways for private individuals to achieve powerful results through their giving. The Annual Meeting is a stimulating and enjoyable way to meet principled donors seeking the breakthroughs that can solve our nation's greatest challenges.

Breakthrough groups
Our Breakthrough groups—focused program areas—build a critical mass of donors around a topic where dramatic results are within reach. Breakthrough groups become a springboard to help donors achieve lasting effects from their philanthropy. Our specialized staff of experts helps grantmakers invest with care in areas like anti-poverty work, philanthropy for veterans, and family reinforcement. The Roundtable's K-12 education program is our largest and longest-running Breakthrough group. This network helps donors zero in on today's most promising school reforms. We are the industry-leading convener for philanthropists seeking systemic improvements through competition and parental choice, administrative freedom and accountability, student-centered technology, enhanced teaching and school leadership, and high standards and expectations for students of all backgrounds. We foster productive collaboration among donors of varied ideological perspectives who are united by a devotion to educational excellence.

A powerful voice
The Roundtable's public-policy project, the Alliance for Charitable Reform (ACR), works to advance the principles and preserve the rights of private giving. ACR educates legislators and policymakers about the central role of charitable giving in American life and the crucial importance of protecting philanthropic freedom—the ability of individuals and private organizations to determine how and where to direct their charitable assets. Active in Washington, D.C., and in the states, ACR protects charitable giving, defends the diversity of charitable causes, and battles intrusive government regulation. We believe the capacity of private initiative to address national problems must not be burdened with costly or crippling constraints.

Protection of donor interests
The Philanthropy Roundtable is the leading force in American philanthropy to protect donor intent. Generous givers want assurance that their money will be used for the specific charitable aims and purposes they

believe in, not redirected to some other agenda. Unfortunately, donor intent is usually violated in increments, as foundation staff and trustees neglect or misconstrue the founder's values and drift into other purposes. Through education, practical guidance, legislative action, and individual consultation. The Philanthropy Roundtable is active in guarding donor intent. We are happy to advise you on steps you can take to ensure that your mission and goals are protected.

Must-read publications

Philanthropy, the Roundtable's quarterly magazine, is packed with useful and beautifully written real-life stories. It offers practical examples, inspiration, detailed information, history, and clear guidance on the differences between giving that is great and giving that disappoints.

We also publish a series of guidebooks that provide detailed information on the very best ways to be effective in particular aspects of philanthropy. These guidebooks are compact, brisk, and readable. Most focus on one particular area of giving—for instance, how to improve teaching, charter-school expansion, support for veterans, programs that get the poor into jobs, how to invest in public policy, and other topics of interest to grantmakers. Real-life examples, hard numbers, first-hand experiences of other donors, recent history, and policy guidance are presented to inform and inspire thoughtful donors.

The Roundtable's *Almanac of American Philanthropy* is the definitive reference book on private giving in our country. It profiles America's greatest givers (historic and current), describes the 1,000 most consequential philanthropic achievements since our founding, and compiles comprehensive statistics on the field. Our *Almanac* summarizes the major books, key articles, and most potent ideas animating U.S. philanthropy. It includes a 23-page timeline, national poll, legal analysis, and other crucial—and fascinating—finger-tip facts on this vital piece of American culture.

Join the Roundtable!

When working with The Philanthropy Roundtable, members are better equipped to achieve long-lasting success with their charitable giving. Your membership in the Roundtable will make you part of a potent network that understands philanthropy and strengthens our free society. Philanthropy Roundtable members range from Forbes 400 individual givers and the largest American foundations to small family foundations and donors just beginning their charitable careers. Our members include:

- Individuals and families
- Private foundations
- Community foundations
- Venture philanthropists
- Corporate giving programs
- Large operating foundations and charities that devote more than half of their budget to external grants

Philanthropists who contribute at least $100,000 annually to charitable causes are eligible to become members of the Roundtable and register for most of our programs. Roundtable events provide you with a solicitation-free environment.

For more information on The Philanthropy Roundtable or to learn about our individual program areas, please call (202) 822-8333 or e-mail main@PhilanthropyRoundtable.org.

ABOUT THE AUTHOR

Joanne Florino is vice president of philanthropic services for the Philanthropy Roundtable. She is also a consultant to the Atlantic Philanthropies Archives at Cornell University.

Ms. Florino has worked in philanthropy for over 35 years. Previously, she was executive director of the Triad Foundation in Ithaca, New York, from April 2003 through March 2013. She was also executive director of the Park Foundation and a program associate at Atlantic Philanthropies.

Ms. Florino was previously vice president of public policy for the Philanthropy Roundtable, served as a strategy committee member for the Alliance for Charitable Reform, chaired the public-policy committee of Grantmakers Forum of New York, and served as a member of the Ethics and Practices Committee of the Council on Foundations. She currently serves as a board member of the Legacy Foundation in Ithaca, New York, the Network of Enlightened Women, and the New York Council of Nonprofits.

Ms. Florino earned a bachelor's degree in history from Georgetown University and a master's degree in American history from Cornell University.